HOW TO CRAFT YOUR CHAPTER

A GUIDE FOR HIGH-PERFORMING MEN TO DISCOVER MEANING (AND JOY) IN RETIREMENT

MICHAEL F. KAY

How to Craft Your Chapter X:
A Guide for High-Performing Men
to Discover Meaning (and Joy) in Retirement
© Copyright 2026 Michael F. Kay

Book design: Clarity Designworks

ISBN 979-8-9943001-0-7 (paperback)
ISBN 979-8-9943001-1-4 (ebook)

LCCN: 2025928097

Disclaimer: This book is provided for general educational purposes only. It is not a substitute for professional advice, diagnosis, or treatment. If you have concerns about your emotional, mental, or physical health, please consult a qualified clinician.

Praise for *How to Craft Your Chapter X*

"*How to Craft Your Chapter X* is a clear, honest guide for high-performing men who feel unmoored in retirement. Michael Kay shows that meaning is not something we lose, but something we realign by leveraging our core values."

—John P. Weiss, author of *The Morning Fox*

"Michael F. Kay offers a hugely helpful and personal guide for men who find the transition from full-time work to retirement challenging, nerve-racking, and even bewildering. By sharing his advice and life experiences as well as wise counsel from men living through "Chapter X," he offers perspective and insights unlike those found in most other books about retirement."

—Richard Eisenberg, "The View From Unretirement" columnist at MarketWatch

"Michael Kay's guide for high-performing men to discover meaning and fun in retirement is invaluable for people considering stopping their career working for money or for those who already have retired and might still be struggling. It's a well-written and well-organized book, upbeat, encouraging, and realistic. Michael refers to his personal experiences as well as shares stories from clients. Several chapters are written by other professionals, which add additional insights. The many exercises and a few visualizations allow the reader to reshape, restructure, realign, and reimagine their future life."

—Rand Selig, author of *Thriving! How to Create a Healthier, Happier, and More Prosperous Life*

"Like the Olympic Games, professional careers celebrate one's ability to strive. But what happens when the striving stops? Letting go, reimagining, and reinventing ourselves beyond our career identity is hard. *How to Craft Your Chapter X* brings simplicity and joy to a process that engages our next chapter of creativity, connection, and growth. I wish I would have had Michael as a guide when I transitioned out of the Olympic world. But I am grateful to have *How to Craft Your Chapter X* at this new stage of life."

—Joe Jacobi, Olympic Gold Medalist, executive coach and author

"I heartily endorse Michael Kay's recommendations for putting together a happy, successful retirement. Many retirees struggle with issues such as loss of status; they may feel the anxiety of no longer having the same sense of purpose. Michael encourages us to think of retirement not as a dreaded endpoint or an extended vacation, but rather as an opportunity to transition to a new set of rewarding activities that fit our values and interests.

"*How to Craft Your Chapter X* is an excellent book, with each chapter offering helpful insights regarding how to objectively evaluate our situation post-career and then to develop a plan. Michael's recommended approach offers a set of core principles (e.g., taking Purposeful Action, adopting a Growth Mindset), utilizes helpful exercises and frameworks like the Wheel of Retirement, and includes extremely useful "guest articles" like "Aging Backwards" by Philip Pape. Overall, it reminds me very much of *What Color Is Your Parachute?*— that venerable guidebook for navigating the challenges of one of life's earlier transitions, choosing a career and searching for a job."

—Ken Mifflin, management consultant

"I have been lucky enough to know Michael for the last 30 years, not simply as a financial advisor, but a true guide for his clients' lives. When Michael retired, we chatted over the process itself and tried to understand what is next for him. Now, over seven years later, he has taken the wisdom and knowledge he had in counseling thousands of clients through all phases of their lives and boiled it into a usable compendium of information to help people like us to think not about "retiring," but to actively and meaningfully write our own next chapter. Michael truly is writing *the* book on our Chapter X, and we are all the beneficiaries of his amazing body of work. Cheers and here's to getting busy living!"

—Alex Potts, President Emeritus, Buckingham Asset Management, Founder, MCAP Ventures, LLC

"*How to Craft Your Chapter X* is a finely tuned process that uses real-life lessons and sound principles to help you develop a more personal and meaningful transition."

—Robert Laura, Founder, Retirement Coaches Association

"Michael Kay has written a comprehensive 'first aid kit' for those entering their post-career life. The thinking exercises provide a mental workout for exploring the road ahead. The stories from Chapter X participants make the advice and counsel more compelling. A must-read for anyone thinking about the Third Half of their life."

—Campbell Gerrish, Third Half Advisors

"Michael Kay cuts through the noise with a clear, compassionate roadmap for navigating one of the biggest demographic shifts of our time: the transition into post-career life. *How to Craft Your Chapter X* gives men the tools to rethink identity, purpose, and connection in an era where longevity is rewriting the rules. Michael brings heart, honesty, and hard-won wisdom to a life stage that deserves far more attention—and far better guidance."

—Bradley Schurman, author of *The Super Age: Decoding our Demographic Destiny*

"As someone who worked as a psychotherapist for many years and has taught conscious aging programs since the late 1990s, I've had a close-up look at how confused and distressed many high-functioning men feel as they approach the post-career phase of their lives. I wish I'd had a map as clear, creative and enjoyable as Michael Kay's *How to Craft Your Chapter X* to give them. This highly accessible guidebook is both practical *and* visionary. It's filled with an amazing blend of down-to-earth information, poignant stories of real people, and hands-on experiential exercises. With this book in hand, you will have everything you need for a richly meaningful and deeply satisfying 'Act III' in your life."

—David Chernikoff, author of *Life, Part Two: Seven Keys to Awakening with Purpose and Joy as You Age*

"*How to Craft Your Chapter X* is a powerful reminder that the stories shaping our lives often run quietly in the background—unquestioned, yet profoundly influential. Michael Kay invites us to bring these stories into the light, to become more self-aware, and to recognize that who we are is not fixed but continually evolving. He shows that retirement is not an ending but a long, unfolding process of rediscovery, taken one thoughtful phase at a time.

"Michael offers a compassionate and practical guide for reimagining identity, meaning, and purpose in the next chapter of life. He reminds us that purpose doesn't have to be grand; it simply has to be ours. Through learning, connecting, and serving others each day, we can cultivate joy and fulfillment no matter what changes come our way.

"This book encourages readers to consciously step into their future and to consider who they are the day before retirement and who they want to become the day after. With wisdom and warmth, *How to Craft Your Chapter X* provides a roadmap for building community, embracing growth, and reframing life with intention."

—Dr. Corinne Auman, author of *Keenagers: Telling a New Story about Aging*

Dedication

To Wendy . . . with love and gratitude.
From One South Ave to now . . .
and the journey continues . . . .

Contents

Introduction

I'll let you in on a secret: I've just finished writing all the chapters of the book, even the conclusion. Now I'm faced with the daunting task of writing the introduction and considering how to usher you into the journey that will begin once you turn to Chapter 1. I'm currently spending a week with my family at the Jersey Shore, where my three granddaughters are having a blast, and my children are enjoying each other's company. My wife and I walk in the morning, greeted by strangers who are similarly walking or riding their bicycles. The age range seems to be from infancy to the late 80s; it's a community of strangers united by the sun, sand, and ice cream. I am thrilled to have everyone together; it makes me so happy.

As we walked toward Barnegat Light House, I envisioned the lighthouse sending out a beacon to help guide ships to safety during storms: a source of power, burning through the mist. Maybe this book can be that source of light for you as you navigate the unknowable seas of change as you transition from your work life to the post-career phase of your life—what I call Chapter X, the name I've given this time of life where you have the opportunity to reshape, restructure, and reimagine what lies ahead. But I want to alert you right at the outset: this light is to show you the rocks and other obstacles; it cannot *prevent* the potential hazards that change portents. But fear not, the light also shines brightly on all the amazing and wonderful possibilities that lie ahead.

I wrote this for high-performing men who have devoted their work lives with a hard-driving, razor-sharp focus on success. It doesn't matter whether you've occupied the CEO's chair, been a world-renowned surgeon or super-lawyer, or created and ran a successful business. It doesn't matter whether you're married, single, divorced, gay, straight, or widowed. What matters is that you bring an open-minded attitude and a desire to create a meaningful pathway to living the next part of your life—with purpose and on purpose. After all, you've been living purposefully for as long as you can remember. But don't get hung up on what your new purpose will be—you'll have a better idea after you've finished the book.

Whether you've already taken the step away from work or retirement is on the horizon, I will show you—actually, this book will help you show yourself—that you already have the tools you need to successfully make the shift. But the work won't be easy. I will walk you through exercises that will require a focused, serious, and committed approach. I am going to ask you to go deep, get real, and kiss reality on or near the lips. Now is not the time to flinch. This transition, without the proper mindset, preparation, and execution, can be less than welcoming. Think of a giant bucket of icy water being poured over your exposed body. I don't want to scare you as to the threats to your emotional and physical well-being (well, actually, I do, at least a little). This is not a change to be treated lightly. The good news is that with the right attitude, awareness, and preparation, you can smooth over the rough spots and enjoy the ride. This book will help you do that.

I created Chapter X (X as in something to solve for in a math equation) as a platform to help men transition to life after their careers.

As I'll detail later in the book, my own post-career transition was rough. I thought I was prepared—turned out I wasn't. During my decades as a financial life planner, I witnessed a similar difficulty that many successful men experience as they wrestle with the loss of identity, the insecurity of finding meaning and purpose, and the challenge of defining who they are when they no longer have a job. Women, by and large, don't have the same difficulty. They seem to move into their new iteration, no longer engaged in their career, with greater ease. This is not an absolute; some women struggle too. But as a man, I don't feel qualified to usher women through their particular challenges.

I began Chapter X with blogs, then added a monthly Zoom get-together. The goal was to provide a safe space for sharing thoughts and ideas. I insisted that we not talk politics or sports. I didn't want the distractions that would take us away from real conversation. Slowly but surely, the community grew and momentum was gained. The marketing expert I worked with during my career, Rochelle Moulton, encouraged me to do a podcast. I initially resisted but eventually succumbed to her brilliant idea. I now see the podcast as an opportunity to bring as many voices forward as possible. Having become a Certified Life Coach, I offered coaching to those seeking a pathway. Lastly, I created a workshop and a keynote to bring the Chapter X message to more men. It was a progression of activities that I hoped would be beneficial to those looking for a clear way forward, and now I have translated everything I have learned (so far) into this book.

What *Is* Retirement?

Before proceeding, I guess we ought to tackle a big question a lot of people have these days. Retirement: What does that even mean anymore? In my childhood, retirement was exemplified by my grandfather. He sat in his comfortable chair, listened to opera, and enjoyed his afternoon schnapps. As I grew older and my father retired, he buried himself in the basement repairing stringed instruments (something he learned to do after he stopped working). He was very involved with his two eldest grandsons, who were living with my parents at the time. My uncle, upon his retirement, continued to teach trombone, traveled a bit, and meticulously took care of his Jaguar XK. While none of their particular activities ring my bell, I recognize that everyone gets to make their choices. My goal is to help you kick open the door to possibilities that reflect your values and provide meaning and purpose (to you)! The fact is, we are not going to be on this earth forever; therefore, each of us gets to determine how we use our allotted time in the most joyful way possible.

During my decades of work as a financial life planner, I've heard a full spectrum of answers to "What does retirement look like to you?" The winner by far was, "I'm gonna play golf." Which is the same thing as saying, "I have no clue." But we are presented with a conundrum. We are living longer, which leaves a longer runway to navigate, added to the pressure of relinquishing power and control to the next generation.

Retirement doesn't need to be the cessation of work. It doesn't need to be 365 days a year of Sundays. Nor does it mean that the rest of your natural days need to be spent balls to the wall, working like a rookie trying to make their bones. It can be a combination of work, play, travel, relaxation, exploration, learning, volunteering, creating, and anything else you conceive of that makes life full and meaningful (to you). *You* get to define what is important to you in creating your next chapter.

Problems arise when you go to your default—aka the least stressful—choice. It's so easy to just keep doing what you're doing than to figure out how to navigate the upheaval of the transition. Then you get stuck—and unhappy about your life.

The decisions necessary in moving forward need to be carefully considered, and that's what I've tried to do in this book: to provide you with a means and method to craft your next chapter. In order to make this guidebook meaningful, you will need to slowly, carefully, and thoughtfully read the chapters and work through the exercises. Patience and focus are required. Some of the exercises are fairly simple and easy and won't tax your brain too much, while others will, most likely, leave you feeling stretched. Give yourself the gift of time to ponder, contemplate, and reflect deeply. Your willingness to invest this time and concentration will pay off greatly as you embark into the newest iteration of you.

How to Use This Book

The book is divided into three sections, which will challenge your thinking, provide information, test your resolve, and make you think deeply about your identity, values, and legacy. There are exercises that will ask you to reflect on your past, consider your experiences, think about your life during retirement, and imagine a future that is filled with meaning and joy. I caution you now, especially when you are digging into the exercises, to tackle the material in this book when you are feeling focused, strong, and committed to the probing questions it asks. In addition to these exercises, I have enlisted the help of four experts who have contributed sections on physical health, mental health, exercise, and the perspective of women, whose role as spouses cannot and should not be discounted during this very challenging life stage.

At the end of most chapters you'll find pieces written by members of the Chapter X community who volunteered to add their thoughts on the transition to life after career. Some work part-time, some are entirely focused on other endeavors and activities that light them up, while others are still exploring and discovering. These pieces, which are labeled "A View from

Chapter X," are not necessarily connected with the chapters they follow. I consider each contribution a piece of wisdom. It might not be yours or mine, but I believe it's essential to understand that there is a vast range of experiences associated with moving into the post-career stage of life.

In addition, the last part of the book contains four chapters from experts: a gerontologist, an exercise specialist, a psychologist, and a therapist who specializes in couples (an oft-ignored topic). I am grateful for their additions, which add valuable insight to the Chapter X experience.

It's a point of emphasis in this book that *you've got this*. You've been through plenty of challenges in this life, tough projects or changes at work, and difficult family issues. You've developed the strength and resilience to handle hard things. The tools are all there. Moving into Chapter X is simply your latest big challenge.

The thrust of this book is to take what you already know and then provide the time and space to evaluate, reflect, and reframe your fears, concerns, and reticence so you can move forward into your next chapter with confidence and strength. I am not intimating that this transition is easy—in fact, it's not. But it is—if you consider the challenges you've already experienced in life—a manageable one. I believe this is a monumental and meaningful transition that offers the opportunity to experience a new phase of life, which, while different, remains important and purposeful.

PART 1
RECLAIMING YOURSELF

CHAPTER 1

Who Am I When I Am No Longer My Title?

"I always likened retirement to falling off a cliff, and then you have to kind of brush yourself off."
—Steve Young, quarterback

Dr. H. and I had been working on his retirement plan since the day he and his wife first came to see me about their financial plan. No, this isn't a book about money and finances. Finances are important, of course, but that big topic is beyond the scope of this book—plus, there are already plenty of great resources on the subject, and my guess is you've devoted a fair amount of energy thus far in making sure you have financial security. Dr. H., an oral surgeon, was contractually due to relinquish his ownership shares at a specified date. He had done a good job of accumulating wealth and, with a few adjustments, everything looked good.

The bulk of our conversation was focused on understanding what his post-career life would look like. As he was approaching his 70th birthday, he was concerned with how he would fill his life. He has lots of ideas and passions. For example, he was an avid fisherman, dedicated to keeping fit, spending time with his grandchildren, and enjoying his second home in Connecticut. He and his wife enjoyed traveling, but didn't want to be constantly on the go. The call of the river and solitude was what truly drew his attention.

The day came, and Dr. H. eased his way into retirement. I felt good that our time together had given him a glide path into his next chapter, along with a sense of comfort, both from the financial and lifestyle points of view. I was optimistic that, with good health, he and his family would be enjoying a full and rich life after his decades of work.

Fast forward six months to our regularly scheduled follow-up meeting.

"So, Tom, how are you and how are you enjoying your new life?" I asked, smiling.

I watched Tom's head tilt down, as if he was making a decision. Then he looked up at me. "I'm working four days a week," he sheepishly responded.

I blinked, not expecting his response. After all, during our many discussions together, he had never said a word about his desire to work part-time after he left.

"Really? Tell me more."

There was a long pause as he decided how to admit that all the planning and strategizing we'd done leading up to his retirement was flushed down the toilet.

"Well," he began, "things started great. I had a pretty good routine going. I went to the gym, I spent some time fishing, but after being home for a few months, I decided that I really missed work. I felt adrift, basically. I was just another old guy on the row of treadmills filled with other old guys. I felt lost, so I started asking around and found an opportunity to fill in for docs who are either sick or away and continued doing surgery."

After gathering my thoughts, I did not alter the smile on my face. I responded, "I'm so glad you are enjoying that, Tom, but

I am curious. You never talked about this as even a possibility. What changed?"

I saw the pensive look on his face as he decided whether or not to share his thoughts. The level of trust we had brought him to blurt out his truth: "Michael, I've been a *doctor* all my life, I don't want to be a *mister*."

The Flower of Truth Is Hidden Beneath the Weeds

There it was, the cold, brutal, inescapable fact. Dr. H. was unable to separate who he was as a person from the title he'd borne for decades, a title that encompassed his sense of being, ego gratification, and identity.

I want you to consider this big question: *Who are you?* It's a question I grappled with, a story that I will share in the next chapter. But for now, the question is on the table, and I dare you to pick it up, look at it, smell it, feel it, taste it, and be with it.

Stepping away from your career, whether by choice or not, comes with a boatload of potential obstacles that you might be confronted with, and your loss of identity is just one. In addition to a loss of identity, you might find:

- loss of purpose
- social isolation
- mental health struggles
- relationship adjustments
- lack of structure
- health decline
- fear of irrelevance
- financial insecurity or uncertainty

I will be talking about each one (except for financial insecurity) throughout the book. Important message! You already have most, if not all, of the tools necessary to climb the ladder to a post-career life that can be fulfilling, joyful, and purposeful.

If you're already retired, you might be experiencing some of these issues right now. And if you're approaching retirement or considering this next phase of your life, chances are you'll be confronted with these realities before too long. But—as I've learned from my soon-to-be retired coaching clients—your challenge is that you haven't felt it yet and cannot even imagine it. Rest assured, the items listed above, including and maybe especially the loss of identity, are something that, once confronted, feels like standing on the precipice of a bottomless ravine.

Way back in 2010, when I was working on my first book, *The Business of Life,* I spent many Wednesdays at my local coffee shop, writing. I would see the same group of older men sitting together bitching about their lives, regrets, and dissatisfactions. I couldn't imagine anything worse than being consigned to wearing a Puma tracksuit, drinking mediocre coffee, and grousing about how the barista misspelled their name . . . again. I overheard their unhappiness and boredom, and how they wished that they'd never retired. Retirement wasn't on my personal horizon then, but from the peanut gallery in the coffee shop, it didn't jive with the hopeful, engaged conversations I was having with my clients. But then again, I wasn't talking to them about lack of identity or the other issues that arose like dandelions in spring.

> **"Reality is irrelevant; perception is everything."**
> —*Terry Goodkind, American author*

Just Because You Think It's True Doesn't Make It So

Where do these serious obstacles come from? Good question. I've worked with a lot of men trying to answer it. All I can say for sure is that the answer is complicated. Let's face it—*life* is complicated.

Think about what our society values and the messages we've been taught since our youth:

- "You're only as good as your last success."
- "Winners write history."
- "Money talks."
- "We glorify youth and fear aging."
- "The cream rises to the top."
- "You are what you achieve."
- "Only the strong survive."
- "Second place is the first loser."
- "You can't teach an old dog new tricks."
- "Don't rest on your laurels."
- "Eat or be eaten."

Our society values and celebrates success, titles, money, power, and youth. Our parents exhorted us with messages that nothing supplanted being number one and that being "good enough" wasn't good enough. We were also pressured with messages about picking a career that would provide for financial and social success. Get good grades so you can go to a top school, get a top job, and then fight your way up the ladder. Unfortunately, there were no conversations about the importance of living a well-balanced life. There was no time to "stop and smell the roses."

So what happens after you've climbed into the C-suite, become the world-renowned surgeon, the super lawyer, the top professional recognized for your mastery in your given field? What do you do for an encore? How have you prepared to step into a new chapter in which you're a *mister,* a used-to-be, a retiree?

For many, the default will be to keep working because they can't think of any alternatives that don't fill them with panic. Their exit will come when someone else boots them out, or a medical issue arises that forces their hand. When either of those events occurs, the prospects for a full, rich, and meaningful life are less than sparkling.

I remember sitting with a couple in my office. They owned a successful business that they were in the process of selling. They were financially fine, and the sale was the icing on the cake. When I asked him how he expected to spend his time after he handed over the keys to the new owner, he said, completely seriously, "I'm going to play golf!"

He was genuinely excited by this prospect.

I asked, "Every day? Every week? Every month? Every year?"

At this point, his wife interjected, looking at him as if he had three heads. "You can play golf two days a week, but you're going to get a part-time job two days and volunteer two days. The seventh will be the wild card."

He responded with a curt nod and a "Yes, dear."

Think about it. His business life was structured. He worked five or six days a week, on a set schedule that varied very little. He knew what to expect, and his focus was on areas of his expertise. He had a great relationship with his staff and customers. His life was narrowly defined. His desire to spend his retirement on the golf course was, of course, fanciful, but also a declaration that he hadn't spent a moment really thinking about it. His wife, on the other hand, instinctively knew he needed a structure in place to provide at least a framework for a more balanced life. Yet this had never occurred to him. Why had this gone unnoticed in his thinking?

Think about the progression of your life since childhood. As we become mobile creatures from stationary babies, our world expands. As we learn to speak and understand, our world grows larger. As we are exposed to nature and experiences that light up our senses, we become sponges, anxious to explore, learn, feel, see, and taste, becoming ever more capable. We thirst for knowledge and want to emulate the adults in our lives.

I remember as a young child watching my father shave each morning. He wet his face and applied a coat of lather from the red, blue, and white Barbasol container. His single-blade safety razor scraped against his skin. I asked him if I could shave too. He pressed the top of the pump and a flow of thick white foam appeared on his hand. He put the shaving cream in my hand and told me to apply it as I'd seen him do countless times. He handed me a plastic comb to use as my razor, and I mimicked the act of shaving, moving my jaw left and right and stretching my lip down. Little did I know then that shaving would lose its allure quickly as it became a daily requirement. But then again, when we are young, we cannot imagine what lies ahead. We only have the comprehension of the moment. The same holds true for this transition to Chapter X.

At a certain point in our development, we become imbued with the message that to be successful, we need to become *something*. My father was a sixth-grade teacher and a musician who, as a child of the Depression, knew the value of money and the importance of work. In fact, until his health started failing, he was the consummate doer, always involved in some purposeful project. As a child, if he found me in front of the TV or on the couch, he would quote Newton's law of physics about "things at rest tend to stay at rest; things in motion tend to stay in motion." In other words, get off your ass and do something meaningful.

As you progressed on your life and career trajectory, the once wide lens of curiosity and exploration became ever narrower. The hyper-focus of specialization and success replaced the wide-eyed wonder of youth. The demands of work and family compelled you to narrow the aperture to provide you with the focus necessary to meet the demands of the most important areas of your life.

Fast forward to this moment. If you are already retired, you might have noticed the challenges of redefining yourself in this new iteration. You might have felt untethered by the lack of structure, social connection, purpose, and relevance. If you've yet to step off the merry-go-round, you might notice just how narrow your focus is right now and how many of these issues haven't yet hit your radar screen. The fact is, without recognizing that life, post-career, requires a reorientation of your thinking, you're liable to be a victim of the narrowest of viewpoints where broader thinking is clearly necessary.

Reclaiming Yourself

In the words of American businessman and writer Max De Pree: "We cannot be who we need to be by remaining what we are." If you are to move strongly forward into this new part of your life, you will need to widen your narrow lens to rediscover, redefine, and reimagine your ideas of meaning, purpose, and fulfillment. In a manner of speaking, you'll need to become a child again.

I call this the process of reclaiming who you were. And it's just that, a process. I wouldn't be going out on a limb by saying you've learned dozens, if not hundreds, of processes in your life. You've gone from not knowing to knowing, or as I love to say, from novice to mastery time and time again and again! You were "someone else" many times before you became this version of you. Now it's time to continue the evolution. But before you can be who you need to be next, we've got some work to do. Like a garden after winter, we need to clean up, turn the soil, germinate some seeds, and nurture the plants to bring them into bloom.

You once were bursting with ideas, enthusiasm, passion, creativity, and a sense of humor. Somewhere between then and now, the fun of just playing, thinking, being, and trying new things got winnowed away with the pressures of life and the focus on achievement and success. Do you recall the "helicopter seeds" from maple trees that used to shower down, twirling and spinning in the wind from branch to ground? I remember watching a shower of them during windy days, while my friends and I would pick them out of the air, split them in half, open the seam, and stick them on our noses. We laughed without judging ourselves or anyone else at the fun of it. I want you to reclaim that part of you, that joy, that unrepentant delight of the experience. It's yours for the taking!

Yes, we've been talking about big, uncomfortable changes. Before you panic or, worse, toss this book into the trash, I want to assure you that *you already know what to do.* You've done it before—countless times. My job, during our journey together, is to remind you, nudge you, encourage you, and support you through the process—through every step that's detailed in this book. Retirement is just another transition in a long history of transitions that started when you went from an immobile baby to crawling and hasn't stopped since. I like to call this phase of life "Chapter X" because it's full of discoveries waiting to be made and variables waiting to be solved.

As you work through this book, I will help you recognize the tools you already have and how they are essential for your next steps. And I will introduce you to a few tools that you will want to consider using as you craft your new life. During my decades of work, and in my years developing Chapter X—coaching men in transition, creating workshops that lead men through the process, and speaking with close friends—I have seen men transform their lives once they reframed their identities and redefined success. I have witnessed their new selves surge with energy and confidence as they shed the unneeded bindings from another time in their lives.

I am confident that all you need to succeed is an open mind, a willingness to step into unfamiliar territory (as you've done many times before), and a positive mindset. Let's go!

A VIEW FROM CHAPTER

"My Chapter X Journey" by Bill LePage[1]

I actually thought I had this whole "retirement" thing figured out. I stepped away from work at 55 after a long career in tech and leadership roles, thinking I was ready for the next phase—more time, less stress, no meetings. And for a while, it was great. But after about three years, I realized I wasn't done. I missed the stimulation, the sense of purpose, and honestly, the feeling that I was still contributing.

So I went back to work. Took on another senior role. The work was meaningful, and I enjoyed being part of something bigger again. But a few years in, I felt that familiar tug: Did I really want to keep running this hard? Did I want to spend this stage of life chasing results, or could there be something else?

That's when I found the Advanced Leadership Initiative (ALI) at Harvard—a program designed for people like me who weren't quite ready to hang it up, but wanted to shift from success to significance. ALI gave me the space to step back and really think: What do I care about now? What kind of impact do I want to have?

I took classes, met incredible people of all ages, and built a project focused on delivering mobility—specifically, free wheelchairs—to people who can't afford them. That mission

---

1 This is the book's first "A View from Chapter X" contribution, as described in the introduction.

was personal: my dad was a quadriplegic for 13 years, so I've seen up close what a difference mobility can make.

Now that I've wrapped up the program, I'm not rushing into anything. I'm in what I'd call a reflective pause. I'm thinking more about alignment than achievement—how to invest my time and energy in ways that feel grounded, useful, and fulfilling. Maybe that's board work. Maybe it's mentoring. Maybe it's something entirely unexpected. I'm open.

Chapter X, for me, isn't about retiring. It's about realigning. It's about doing less of what drains me and more of what matters. With a bit more clarity. A bit more freedom. And hopefully, a bit more impact.

CHAPTER 2

. . . .

Unlabeling: How to Recover the Real You

"Be yourself; everyone else is already taken."
—*Oscar Wilde, author and poet*

As I zeroed in on my career departure date, December 31, 2020, I really felt ready. I had spent months pondering this transition and had created a list of "dos and don'ts" describing what I wanted and what I didn't. It was important to me that my analysis reflected how I felt on a gut level. I started with the "Ben Franklin" T-account, which had been a great tool I'd used in decision-making throughout my career. The left side was the pluses, and the right side was the minuses. I divided a blank document into two columns.

My Yeses	My Nos
Staying fit	No financial planning/ financial coaching
Time with friends and family	No strict schedule
Creative endeavors	Limit time on the couch/TV
Exploring new things	Say NO to things that are not joyful

I had begun my exploration by returning to music after a 50—yes, 5-0—year hiatus. I was a classically trained trumpet player in my teens. Still, after years of teacher abuse and the self-created pressure to be the "best," I put my Silver Getzen "Doc" Severinsen model trumpet in the case, determined never to open it again. But after a conversation with a friend who is a world-renowned musician, I decided to reopen the case and started taking lessons. It required me to lose, or at least work on, my perfectionism and focus on just having fun.

During 2020, I was heavily engaged in considering what my life would look like post-career. I had taken several courses to become a certified life coach, feeling that this was a way to align my desire to help others while avoiding discussions or guidance about money. They were intensive courses of study that would finally culminate in the following year.

As I was on the precipice of this monumental change, I created a community for men transitioning to life after career, which I called Chapter X. After decades as a financial planner, I realized that men had the most difficulty in this transition. I figured, "I could offer some guidance and assistance based on my experience as a financial life planner and, now, a certified life coach. Maybe I can make a difference." OK, what's the story with the X? I know you're dying to know. Well, the truth is, it harkens back to my days in Algebra 1, which left me in a deep confusion that remains a miasma of mist around my brain to this day. All I remember is having to solve for X. Therefore, calling it Chapter X seemed like a natural fit as we're all trying to solve the variables for this new chapter of life, for which we have no idea what's in store.

I started Chapter X by writing a daily blog and sending it out to whoever signed up on my new website. I'd gotten some notice from well-known journalist Richard Eisenberg, who was then writing for Next Avenue. With his mention, more and more men signed up for my messages. Five days a week, I would share my thoughts about this transition with the readers, hoping I was hitting the right notes more often than not.

I must admit, as December 31 neared, I was feeling pretty good. I was active, working out four to five days per week, writing, spending time with my granddaughters, practicing trumpet, and actually having fun. I was optimistic.

I woke on January 1, 2021, with a feeling of joy. No, it wasn't a continued buzz from a New Year's Eve party. It was the realization that the journey I had started at 12, with my first job, and continued to the present, 56 years later, was over. I felt great, hopeful, light-hearted, and ready!

In the first several months of 2021, I took on the tasks and to-dos I had outlined. Cleaning and sorting out messes that had accumulated over the years. Making my workspace more comfortable and organized. I was writing, playing music, living my new life. It seemed like everything was falling nicely into place.

And then it all fell apart.

I tried using the "fake it 'til you make it" approach, but it was a shoddy cover-up for how I was feeling. I tried to identify the whens and the wheres of these feelings. The emptiness in the pit of my stomach, the brain fog, the lack of motivation, and the sadness I felt in my heart.

The worst part for me was a double dose of recrimination. I felt that I had not only let myself down, but also those who read my supposed words of wisdom and advice. I looked in the mirror and saw a hypocrite who shamefully wrote uplifting and positive messages to the world but didn't practice them himself. I didn't understand what was happening to me. I knew I just felt terrible.

My solution was to open my heart and pour out my feelings on my blogs. I shared my sense of loss, sadness, and vulnerability. What I got back from the Chapter X community was support, encouragement, and love. People could relate to my feelings, something that often came through strongly in our monthly Zoom meetings. What I came to realize after some time with my therapist and time in contemplation was that I felt untethered to my lifetime of being someone, doing something with purpose, making money, creating a business, nurturing relationships.

In short, I had not mourned the death of my previous life . . . the earlier me. I had been too busy focused on what was next. I had not grieved the loss of the firm I created, which had formed so much of my identity, and the decades of driving, developing, supporting a family, failing, building, and being in charge. There, I said it. I put it all out there for everyone to see the emperor without clothes. I stood naked (forgive the image) for everyone to see.

The Art of Reinvention (How to Reframe Your Life)

The fact is, throughout my career, I had to reinvent myself many times. For example, I went from full-throttle musician (all my focus was here) to becoming an accountant to forsaking my CPA certification to join the financial services industry to realizing that I have no interest in selling insurance or mutual funds to creating my own practice to developing a multi-advisor firm that became a state-of-the-art fee-only planning firm. Each step was a birth and a death. Each iteration of myself included failures, learning, progress, and reinvention. Each phase of life required acquiring new skills, knowledge, attitudes, and habits. Looking back on my many demanding but successful transitions, I realized that, despite the challenges, I had the tools I needed to fully live this next chapter.

Throughout my life, I've had a lot of labels hung on me, some of my own making, some provided by others. Each label brought with it expectations, responsibilities, and both internal and external judgments. Here are some of the labels that spring to mind: son, brother, child, student, "the butcher/bagel boy of Pleasantdale," musician, graduate, fraternity brother, accountant, husband, father, CPA, insurance agent, registered representative, CFP, financial planner, entrepreneur, president, author, speaker, adjunct professor, board member . . . some last forever, others melt away into irrelevance. I guarantee you that I could knock on any door in Pleasantdale and not one person would remember the "butcher/bagel boy"!

I could go on and on, including titles, skills, and experiences that added to my capability to evolve into whom and what I needed to become. With each new label, the past label drops off, although the skillsets remain, and a new set of expectations, challenges, and knowledge is there to master.

The transition from your career to life, after handing in your employee ID card, is huge because, not only are you saying goodbye to all the professional labels you've worked so hard to acquire, but you're also left without a mentor, coach, or model to help you set the table for the next meal to be consumed. This "unlabeling"—which unfairly portrays you as a "use-to-be"—is antithetical to everything on which you've built your life. You are naked and alone in a frozen and desolate landscape with no shelter in sight. Except that's how you *feel*. The reality of your situation is far different. You've been "practicing" for this stage all your life. Now, you just need to make a few adjustments in your thinking.

Here's something that helped me. See if it helps you. I considered the skillsets I'd acquired over the decades:

- Resilience
- Problem-solving
- Learning
- Creativity

- Communication with others
- Flexibility
- Understanding purposeful action

In addition, I focused on my values and how they have helped guide me throughout my life:

- My family
- My health
- My friends and relationships
- Helping others
- Learning new things
- Creativity
- Living joyfully

I realized that the items on these lists were the raw resources at my disposal to reinvent myself—and they were plenty powerful. The time for mourning was over. Now it was time to turn the page to my new chapter with greater strength and a greater understanding. As I thought back over my life, it occurred to me that there was a cycle that had escaped my awareness. That cycle was one of vision. Allow me to clarify. As a child, every new development or change brings a greater and wider perspective. Think about your early life and how curious you were about everything. Each discovery was met with awe, wonder, and learning. I remember as a child trying to free a stuck piece of bread from the toaster. I jammed a knife into the slot and was rewarded with an electric shock that sent me sprawling. Did I mention learning? This was learning at its finest. But as we age and our lives become aimed at something specific—think career—our gaze narrows.

Remember high school, where you took a full range of subjects: math, history, English, foreign language, art, music, gym, geography, etc. Then think about college, where you declared a major. Gone was the wide range of subjects to be sampled; here, the focus narrowed to what was on the required curriculum. If you pursued post-grad education, the focus became even narrower. We went from a wide-angle lens to a narrow focus, and then to a microscope. This tunnel vision was necessary for that stage of life, but did we consider what we might have missed out on along the way?

The good news is that you never lose your ability to rewiden your lens, to learn and adapt and reinvent yourself. To change your identity. Let's move up the years a little. Do you remember your first job? *Of course you do!* Take a moment and put yourself back in time to the morning of your first day at work. Think about how you were feeling, what you were thinking, what you were expecting. Think about walking into the office or place of employment on that first day. *Wow!* I don't know about you, but my accounting degree felt about as useless as a worn-out sneaker. One thing is clear: I was excited, open, nervous, optimistic, and ready to take it all in!

Ten years later, when I left public accounting, the excitement, the enthusiasm, and the optimism had waned. As I gained experience, my focus fell into several areas: I was an audit manager and was engaged in forensic accounting. These areas were very narrow and specific.

When I transitioned to financial services, I knew very little (almost nothing), and again, my lens was wide open to learn everything. Throughout the decades of growth, change, failures, and development, my focus narrowed again to the specifics of my specialty as a financial life planner.

What about life outside of a career? Think about how your lens shifts when you enter a relationship, get married, and have a family. Chances are that your life lens went from wide open to microscopic as the pressures of career, family, and life increased. There just aren't enough hours in the day to take on more than what's on your overflowing plate. Maybe now is a good time for you to start identifying these experiences in your life and to consider how you might reframe your thinking about your future and your view of the world. We're going to dig deeply into this exercise in Part 2 of the book, but beginning to think along these lines is a good way to, as they say, prime the pump.

Recently, I ran into a young man (in his 40s) whom I'd come to know over the years. He asked me about my life now, and I shared some of what I'm doing. He looked at me with wonder and said, "Between work and taking the girls to their activities, I barely have time to play a round or two of golf a year." It tracks.

So here we are. Whether you are on the path to your Chapter X or already in it, you will need to confront and come to terms with the thoughts and feelings you have around your identity, the tools you possess but might not have realized you have, and your values. In the coming chapters, I'll be introducing additional tools to help you grow into your new phase of life, but not just yet. We'll get there.

In the next chapter, we'll start by delving more deeply into values and a few exercises that can help you really home in on what your "musts" are going forward. Meanwhile, to juxtapose Stephen Covey, I'd like you to begin with the beginning in mind.

A VIEW FROM CHAPTER X

"Finding New Purpose" by Andy Abrahams

Like I was in my working life, I've been a late bloomer in Chapter X, too. I didn't want to stop working at age 61, but apparently, whatever I was trying to sell to other employers, they weren't buying. So I was fortunate to be able to retire, and while I was happy to leave a job and place of work I didn't like, I wasn't prepared for life on the other side.

I was lost during the first year of retirement. The hours and days unfolded, and I loved playing golf when I wanted to and taking little jaunts. But I was a bit rudderless, so I knew I had to make more of an effort.

I joined Chapter X and enjoyed learning others' views on the back nine of life. Slowly but surely, I became intentional about using my vast amounts of free time in meaningful and fulfilling ways. I started by volunteering more at City Harvest, the food rescue organization in New York, and I eventually became a shift leader at green markets across the city. I loved the feeling that I got from doing my small part to help fill an elemental need in people's lives. But I also found a new cohort, my fellow volunteers, bonded by a desire to do good.

I'm not sure how much more wisdom I've accumulated, but I have found a contentment most days that feels like a life well lived. I'm also acutely aware of how lucky I am to have relatively good health so far and the ability to live a reasonably comfortable life. The addition of our first granddaughter has also been a never-ending source of joy, and I love being the patriarch of a loving family.

PART 2

WHO ARE YOU? AND WHAT'S REALLY IMPORTANT?

CHAPTER 3

Reconnecting with Your Core Identity

"In a world where you can be anything,
be yourself."
—*Albert Einstein, physicist*

Your journey began at birth . . . my how you've grown! While you were still an eating and pooping machine in the crib, your personality and belief structure began to be formed. Your responses to stimuli informed your behavior. Hard fact: very little has changed over the decades of your life. Over your lifespan, you have continued to adapt, grow, learn, refine, and accumulate your beliefs, behaviors, and habits.

The learning process helps us to hold on to or discard unneeded pieces that no longer support us. Do you remember casting off the crayon in favor of the pencil? Or maybe snail mail for email? I remember when, in college, I got my first handheld calculator, which made life a little easier. During my first job as an accountant, the "old timers" would chide the "new kids" for using a calculator, claiming it would only diminish their ability to, as they prided themselves, *do it in their heads.* Yeah, big deal!

In other words, change happens. While change, when we initiate it, seems to be easier to grasp, that which is forced upon us is typically met with resistance. After decades of creating an identity, a life purpose, a passion, and a reason to get out of bed in the morning, facing Chapter X, with all those support structures and routines stripped away, can be, to say the least, traumatic.

Whether you have already crossed the threshold to this next part of life or are approaching it, you can see that this challenge is monumental unless you have gone through a process of reorientation, thoughtful research, practice, self-awareness, and evaluation. I have had countless conversations with men who have walked the tightrope from successful careers to lives where work is either ceased entirely or plays an insignificant role. I know many men who have dived into the chasm of despair and misery for a myriad of reasons. One of the biggest reasons is the often-relied-on Ready, Fire, Aim approach. That doesn't work in business, and it's not going to work so well in other parts of your life either. I think you get the picture.

The purpose of this book is to introduce you to the many challenges that lie ahead and provide you with tools that will help you focus on what you need to do to move forward successfully. For example, before you start running around and signing up for fourteen post-graduate courses, you might want to start with the basics.

When I say "the basics," I am focusing on your limiting beliefs, your identity, and your core values. That's the stuff we'll be tackling in Part 2. As we make progress in those areas, we will focus on the key idea of heightening your self-awareness so that you can decide how to use the precious time you've been allotted. Allow me to put this in very stark terms. A study published in the *Journal of the American Medical Association* stated that a man who retires at age 70 has approximately 9 million minutes left.[2] That's 545 million seconds. Tick, tick, tick . . . .

Of those 9 million minutes, if you take away time to sleep and eat, you're now down to 5.3 million minutes. Again, tick, tick, tick . . . . If your final three years are filled with cognitive and or physical decline, you're now down to 4.4 million minutes or 8.34 years. Do I need to put a finer point on this pencil?

Reframing Your Life

Throughout the book, I will introduce you to the information I share with workshop attendees and those I coach one-on-one. There will be worksheets to provide you with the focus to think about and record your observations and ideas, and to help you begin to create a game plan. Think of it like a business plan for your next chapter that provides you with a deep sense of meaning, purpose, and, dare I say, *fun!*

The Chapter X program is a proven process that will enable you to discard beliefs, behaviors, and habits that no longer serve you well in this stage of your life. In place of those, you will learn to adapt to your new reality, acquire the necessary skills, and decide what will fill your life with meaning and purpose based on how *you* define those terms. I've heard from men who get stuck on the idea of meaning and purpose. They trip all over the idea that it needs to be "big," it needs to "change the world," it needs to be "seismic!" But nothing can be further from the truth. What you believe the external world thinks is completely a construct

---

2 A comprehensive study published in the *Journal of American Medical Association* (JAMA) in 2016, titled "The Association Between Income and Life Expectancy in the United States, 2001–2014," was conducted by a team of researchers led by Raj Chetty from Stanford. It found that the life expectancy for men in the top 1% of the income distribution range had an expected age of death of 87.3 years.

of your imagination. I suggest it's time to stop worrying about or considering the imagined judgments of others. The reality is, *you* get to decide what provides meaning and what is purposeful *to you*.

For some, meaning and purpose revolve around time with grandchildren; for others, it might be helping out at a food bank or working in a community garden. It might mean mentoring a young entrepreneur or spending time visiting friends who are sick. It might mean learning new skills or picking up a musical instrument after a 50-year hiatus. It could mean a combination of all these things, and maybe a few more. But discovering your meaning and purpose involves first understanding your identity, and then defining or redefining your core values.

After decades of work and a lifetime of focusing on success, you will need a new set of metrics to define success and achievement. Endless hours of striving for the gold ring and climbing the endless ladder ever upward have led to a cortisol-infused, exhausted exit into a new chapter of life where you lack the framework, mindset, and direction in which to orient yourself. As discussed in Chapter 1, your lens, which, for all your adult life, has been ever-narrowing, is now a pinhole. You've gone from novice to mastery many times since childhood. You are about to enter a stage where you are stripped of all the badges, honors, accolades, and recognition you have worked so hard to accrue. Your expensive suits hang idly in the closet like forlorn ghosts of another era, and the Puma track suit awaits. It's just you, naked and alone, and back at novice.

OK, so it might not really be that dire. After all, you have a lifetime's experience dealing with change, and you're probably pretty good at it now. I just want you to recognize that after a lifetime of working for success, you have another big challenge ahead. And this one's quite a bit different from the ones you've dealt with before. But it *is* one where you have most of the tools to move forward boldly. It's a matter of reorientation, reframing, and letting go.

So what's the first step? Let's start with some reframing.

But first, an important note: I cannot stress enough the importance of identifying and leaning into your "tribe" as you go through the exercises in this book. Your spouse, partner, relatives, and friends can be great sounding boards to help you test your thinking. Just keep in mind that, like all of us, those good people may have their own personal prejudices or attitudes that might shade their thinking and counsel. So while those who know you best can offer great support and advice, remember that it also must match up with what your heart tells you—especially after you've gone through the intensive introspection and reflection that these exercises require.

Reframe: Who Do You Think You Are?

When I think back over my lifetime, I've held a lot of titles. I mentioned a number of them in Chapter 2. After thinking about it a bit, I can expand that list to include nephew, cousin, neighbor, friend, camper, school patrol, dog-sitter, helper—all before age 12. Then came the kid who worked in the butcher shop, was a trumpet student and player, a writer for the school paper, a student conductor, and a high school graduate. Then college happened, where I became an accounting student, roommate, boyfriend (where I met my future wife), bookstore clerk, grocery store worker, car parker, admissions office clerk, construction worker, glass factory worker, bookkeeper, intern, and college graduate. Then I became a CPA, husband, father, coach, Board of Education member, Planning Board member, financial services representative, CFP®, father-in-law, financial life planner, author, speaker, entrepreneur, employer, colleague, mentor, grandparent (papa) . . . .

Odds are good that you've got an analogous list. The many titles we've worn are important in how we identify ourselves and how others identify us. They become who we are. We embody each and wear them like a second skin. But here's a fact: while the experiences of each of those titles in my list added to who I am, none of them truly define me, perhaps except for husband, father (in-law), and papa.

You might have had the title of CEO, MD, JD, or any of countless other identifiers of your training, accomplishments, and success, but none of those titles is who you are. If you think back to Dr. H. in the first chapter, he just couldn't see himself as anything other than a *doctor*. The idea of being a *mister* was just too high a hurdle for him to climb over.

How do you define yourself? I have attended social functions where many of the men are no longer engaged in their careers, and frankly, the bulk of the conversation centered on war stories from their careers. As you step into your Chapter X, ask yourself the fundamental question: Who am I? The answer to that question is what will populate the road ahead with a number of helpful guideposts. We'll dig deeper into this with a formal exercise in Chapter 4. For now, allow these thoughts to enter your bloodstream and move around in your body.

Limiting Beliefs

Your identity is just one area where you might have a limiting belief, similar to Dr. H. Limiting beliefs keep us stuck in a particular place or time and prevent us from becoming who we need to be to live full, rich, and meaningful lives. I recently spoke with someone who declared that he is an athlete, based on his passion for cycling, skiing, and other physical activities. Unfortunately, after he suffered an accident that left him unable to participate in any meaningful (to him) activity, he felt lost, disconnected, and miserable. He allowed his own limiting belief to back him into a corner, leaving no outlet for escape.

Your identity isn't the only thing affected by limiting beliefs. During my experience in working with men, these are some of the most prevalent messages:

- I no longer have a purpose.
- I was put on this earth to work, make money, and be productive.
- The end of work is the end of life.
- I am not relevant.
- I have hit my peak. What's left to look forward to?
- Retirement happens *to* us; someone else will control the outcome.
- If I am not constantly busy and focused, I am not being a "good" person.
- I can't change at this age.
- Happiness in retirement is all about money.
- It's selfish to focus on myself now.
- No one will want to connect with me outside of my work networks.
- It's too late to make a difference or leave a legacy.
- I should be able to figure this all out alone.

Do any of these feel uncomfortably familiar? I can assure you, they've cropped up many times in Chapter X discussions. Can you think of any that aren't on the list? Jot down any of these beliefs that resonate or feel true. We're going to dig into them later.

Facts are facts. The end of your work denotes a significant intellectual and emotional shift, as certain aspects of your life are lost in their present form: social connection, ego gratification, professional challenge, and routine (and you know how much we *love* our routines, even if we rail against them). But let's get real. There was a time in your life when you couldn't imagine not playing with your Erector Set or Tinker Toys, but you survived, right? You grew into something greater. I'm excited to see what's in store for you next.

Self-Awareness: The Master Virtue

Before we move on to the next chapter, I want to spend some time talking about self-awareness, which I consider to be the master virtue to develop because it undergirds everything else in the Chapter X program. Self-awareness is one of those things we all believe we possess in abundance. Unfortunately for most of us, this isn't true—at least not on a regular basis. We all have blind spots. We all have trouble really seeing ourselves consistently. There are many reasons for this, but I will focus on the major one: cognitive biases clouding our perception.

Cognitive biases might be the most prevalent saboteurs of self-awareness. They come in a wide variety, and everybody suffers from one or more of them. Some of their many forms include confirmation bias, self-serving bias, and fundamental attribution error. Confirmation bias is the tendency to seek out, interpret, and remember information in a way that confirms what we already believe. We see this commonly in our political choices, in relationships, and in our self-perception. We tend to notice what supports our view, ignore what runs counter to our thinking, remember information that aligns with our existing beliefs, and dismiss or rationalize that which doesn't. It's a slippery slope that very typically escapes our view unless we are intentionally looking. And it can make the transition to the next chapter of your life unnecessarily challenging.

One common cognitive bias is self-serving bias, which allows us to take credit for wins and lay blame for failures squarely on the shoulders of outside forces. It protects our egos and is a great example of a lack of self-awareness. This is all too common in the workplace, where it's easy to put the fault for lack of success in someone else's hands. I imagine you've run into people like that along the way. This reminds me of a man I spoke with who was convinced he wasn't at fault for his lack of success in meeting new people. Then finally, after a long conversation, he admitted to me that his attempts were feeble, at best.

Another bias is the fundamental attribution error. This is the tendency to overemphasize one's personal traits and underemphasize context. You know, like when someone cuts you off and you react in various negative ways. But if you accidentally cut someone off, you might tell yourself that you didn't see them . . . *Ooops!*

Looking inside is, for many, uncomfortable. It means facing feelings that may have been buried or denied, like childhood traumas. Life presents many opportunities to distract us, so that we don't have to look too deeply. It's easier to scroll reels of gym disasters (yeah, they're hilarious) than to really ponder the root causes of how you feel and why, especially since men have been taught to stuff those feelings away. Doing a deep dive into ourselves may challenge lifelong beliefs or identities and make us feel unsafe. But let's get something straight, there's no better time than now to get down to reality and see ourselves and all our flaws. If not now, when?

So much of our behavior is unconscious; it's on autopilot. Who we are in adulthood is shaped by beliefs, memories, emotional patterns, and learned behaviors. We may not be fully aware of them, but they still influence our decisions, identity, and reactions today.

Here's an example from my life. My father grew up in the Great Depression in essentially a single-parent home. Based on his years of experiencing deprivation and financial insecurity, he *hated* spending money. My mother was 11 years younger. While she didn't come from any level of wealth, she never experienced the financial lack my father suffered from. She *loved* spending money. The result was that my parents constantly fought about money. No, I don't mean quiet and polite disagreements!

During my first training as a financial life planner through Money Quotient, there was a deep dive into the impact of our childhood experiences with money. For example, some people looked at their money history and shared that, for them, "money was for fun"; for others, "money was to help others"; and still others thought "money was a tool." This exercise uncovered that, for me, money equaled *conflict*. This realization helped me understand why I was so uncomfortable talking about money with my wife and how I avoided, deflected, and distracted all financial conversations. It wasn't until this introspection that I gained the self-awareness of my behavior and how childhood experiences impacted my life in the present. It was painful, but revelatory and life-changing. I became a better husband and a happier person for the experience.

We absorb so much in our childhood that we are unaware of in adulthood. Our money beliefs are just one example. Think about how we are conditioned to accept certain behaviors, like conformity (we want to fit in) or our gender roles (boys don't cry). We also absorb our ideas of masculinity, achievement, and family roles. But do we ever ask ourselves whether the stories we tell ourselves are true? Rarely, at least unless we intentionally lean into it. Usually, they are operating silently in the background, beyond our immediate awareness. But their existence directs our thinking and behaviors.

If we become aware, we then have the responsibility to change. Right? But we all know that change sucks! It requires discomfort, pain, sleepless nights, and the potential for failure. *Yuck!* Think about starting a weight-lifting regimen: you know the next day, everything hurts. But after a while, the pain goes away as your muscles strengthen and your body adjusts (except after leg days). So, we avoid change wherever possible. After all, who wants to deal with it? Hmm, let's see what's playing on Netflix. Change is messy, uncertain, uncomfortable, and inconvenient. If we are blissfully unaware of the need to change, perhaps we can remain in the status quo! Yay!

To sum it all up, the lack of self-awareness is a slippery slope leading to all manner of potential pitfalls, obstacles, and problems. To put it plainly, you can no longer afford to hide behind a lifetime of comfortable ignorance. Here, on the cusp of a significant change, the transition into your Chapter X, it's time to throw off the yoke of servitude to a false master. I want you to succeed in this new phase of life, and I believe self-awareness is the key. I say this based on years of coaching men embarking on their post-career lives, and from working closely with the Chapter X community. Self-awareness *always* makes the road easier.

Fear not: there are many ways to improve your self-awareness. There are many tools available to help you get better acquainted with the you who has been hiding deep inside, the you who is ready to blossom in this exciting new stage of your life.

It comes down to doing some hard thinking about yourself. There's no avoiding this work. For many, journaling is a great way to start the dive in. It helps to clarify thoughts and emotions, as everything is there in black and white to see and ponder. In fact, it is an act of self-leadership. Some people can just free-write their feelings, while others benefit from using writing prompts, like:

- What am I feeling right now and why?
- What am I avoiding, and what would it mean to face it?
- When do I feel most like myself?

- ✕ What belief is holding me back right now?
- ✕ What am I grateful for?
- ✕ What do I know now that I wish I had known earlier?
- ✕ What does a good day look like?
- ✕ Is that belief really true or just something I've accepted as true?

If you're new to journaling, use a simple notebook and give yourself 5 to 10 minutes a day. Some people prefer to start their day first thing in the morning, while others dig in at the end of the day. Don't worry about grammar, spelling, or sentence structure—this is your safe space to get your ideas and thoughts on paper. It's just for you!

Another self-discovery tool is the Johari Window, which was developed by Joseph Luft and Harrington Ingham in 1955. It contains a grid of four quadrants. The horizontal boxes are labeled "Known to Self" and "Not Known to Self" from left to right. The vertical grids, from top to bottom, are "Known to Others" and "Not Known to Others." The top left open box is "Open Area" (Known to Self and Known to Others). The top right is the "Blind Spot" (Not Known to Self and Known to Others). The bottom left quadrant is labeled "Hidden Area" (Known to Self and Not Known to Others). And the bottom right is "Unknown" (Not Known to Self and Not Known to Others).

The Open Area includes things you share freely, such as strengths, beliefs, feelings, and behaviors that others can observe. The Blind Spot contains aspects that others see in you but you are unaware of: life habits, tone of voice, or other patterns. You know, how others perceive you that you cannot see. The Hidden Area contains things you keep private, like past experiences, emotions, or insecurities. The Unknown Area is filled with the unconscious drivers, latent talents, buried memories, or other things that no one sees or hasn't seen yet. For example, a trauma that subtly shaped your behavior. This area is perhaps the trickiest, as it requires deep reflection, therapy, life experiences, or major life challenges.

The Johari Window can help you clearly visualize how much of you there is to discover. To use this tool, aim to expand the open areas, shrink the blind spots, reveal what is hidden, and explore the unknown. Easy-peasy! OK, maybe not. It's a process. It starts with self-awareness and progresses with intention and practice. Think of it like an archaeological excavation, each layer or level revealing some new information.

It's beyond the scope of this book to delve too much into this subject, but rest assured that there are plenty of other robust and time-tested tools to help develop one's self-awareness. Among these are personality and strengths assessments like MBTI, Clifton Strengths, Big Five, or the Enneagram. Mindfulness and meditation are other paths to self-awareness. There are many apps out there, like Ten Percent Happier, Insight Timer, and Headspace. Quieting the mind and body to relax into yourself is a gift to be explored and expanded.

A VIEW FROM CHAPTER

"My Incomplete Journey Toward Retirement" by Michael Zeldin, PhD

I began my journey toward retirement about 7 years before my official retirement date. Although I left full-time employment 5 years ago, I am still not fully retired. I would describe my retirement process as "phased," and just like in adolescence, I am still going through phases. Let me explain.

I am a professor, and for 15 years I was also an academic administrator, serving as the Senior National Director of the

Schools of Education at a four-campus graduate school. I was responsible for six graduate programs and tens of millions of dollars of grant money. The responsibility was enormous, and the stress never-ending. As I approached age 65, I began thinking about retirement. My financial advisor told me I could retire at any time and I would be well-positioned. So, I did what any good academic does: I began researching retirement, reading any book I could find, consulting with retirement experts, and working with a therapist who could do much more than help me make a list of pros and cons.

She led me through a process of "voice dialogue" where I would move to one side of the Zoom screen to talk to myself about all the reasons I wanted to retire, and then move to the other side to tell myself all the reasons I did not want to retire. Then I returned to the middle of the screen to reflect on what I heard from the two sides of myself.

What became clear was that I was not ready to give up the professorial life I had lived for 40 years, but that I also didn't want to remain in my high-pressure leadership position. So, I decided to create my own phased retirement plan. I stepped down from the administration and returned to my professorial role, focusing on teaching and research. I did this step-down role for 5 years until I officially "retired" at age 70 (thereby making myself eligible for the highest Social Security benefits, which I had earned). I also negotiated a small emeritus package, including a bit of teaching and reading a few students' capstone projects. Teaching keeps my mind engaged and makes sure I stay in touch with people younger than myself. In addition, I accepted a role on the faculty of an education institute that meets twice a year for 4-day retreats.

What have I learned through all this? First, I am tremendously happy with the pared-down schedule and responsibilities. I have time to spend with my grandchildren and partner; I even drive carpool at least once a week, easing my daughter's burden on her busiest days. My partner and I can schedule two to three cruises each year, which we love, along with weekend getaways to local vacation spots.

Second, I learned that I don't have to fill each day to overflowing, but I also can't leave days void of any meaningful activities. Before we retired, we visited my partner's graduate school roommate in a distant city. He had worked in the mental health field for the federal government and retired a few years before we did. I asked him how he filled his days, especially since he had retired relatively early. He told us that as long as he had two meaningful things on his calendar each day (not things like "do the laundry"), his days were filled and fulfilling. I have tried to follow his advice.

Third, I have not entirely detached from my work-life identity. I am still a professor, both in the eyes of others and in my own mind. Perhaps because I stay in touch with alums of the programs I directed, maybe because I am teaching versions of the courses I taught during the most active years of my career, or probably because I'm just wired this way, I still feel connected to my pre-retirement identity. Teresa Amabile and her colleagues, in a wonderful book titled *Retiring: Creating a Life That Works for You*, identify four tasks of retirement: deciding when and how to retire, detaching from work, building a provisional life structure, and consolidating a stable life structure for retirement. Reflecting on where I am as I write this, I have not accomplished the second task (detachment), and right now, I see no urgency to work on it.

I do have a life structure that brings me joy (the outcome of Amabile's fourth task). My partner and I have a comfortable routine punctuated by frequent short trips and several longer cruises each year. I spend time with my grandchildren every week, helping out their parents and bringing joy to the children (and to myself). We have a robust and growing social circle, consisting of long-time friends and those who have come into our lives in recent years. We both have just enough work to keep us stimulated. We have rich spiritual lives through our involvement in three Reform Jewish temples and an Episcopal church.

Here are five lessons I've learned from my incomplete journey that may be useful to those just setting out on the retirement journey:

1. Retiring is a long-term process best taken in phases.

2. The keys to joy and fulfillment in retirement are learning, connecting, and being of service to someone every day.

3. No matter what is going on in the world, maintaining joy is an act of resistance ("We won't let 'them' take our joy away") and is ultimately the key to resilience.

4. Find one or more communities to be part of (spiritual, intellectual, hobby-related, etc.) and participate with regularity.

5. Work every day to strengthen your relationships with those to whom you are closest.

CHAPTER 4

Figuring Out the New You

"Knowing others is intelligence;
knowing yourself is true wisdom."
—*Lao Tzu, Chinese philosopher*

Just as every stage and transition was a death of something, it was also a new beginning. With each stage, you came away with new knowledge, new experience, new ideas, new tools, and new competency. This change is no different. You've built a lifetime of failures, successes, growth, learning, resilience, and knowledge. Now it's time to put all that experience to work.

The last chapter introduced the concepts of core identity and the need to reframe how you think about yourself. Unfortunately, the specter of the limiting beliefs we carry about ourselves requires a hard look, using our self-awareness to battle back these forces that aim to keep us locked in place.

This chapter will challenge you with three exercises that delve into identity and your conception of your life now and in the future. Then we'll pivot to your memories of your first day of work in the real world. I don't know anyone who doesn't love this exercise. Then comes a strong shift to your values. We'll wrap up with a deep dive into regret.

Important note! The exercises in this chapter (in fact, throughout the entire book) are meant to be challenging, so I would like you to be rested and focused for each one of them. That means you don't necessarily need to do them all in one sitting or even in a single day. It's fine to take them slowly. Use whatever approach works best for you to put in your best effort.

This feels like a great place for your first exercise. On the following page is the worksheet you'll be using.

As you can see, there are three questions to be completed here. But first, a word of advice. It is important to actually put pen (or pencil) to paper rather than typing it on the computer. I insist on this when working with coaching clients and in workshops.

Research[3] has shown that handwriting slows you down and helps with reflection, deeper thinking, and emotional processing (vital for this particular exercise). It actually engages different parts of your brain.[4]

Before you put pen to paper, here are a few thoughts: This is the very beginning of your Chapter X journey. Think of it as an exploration. Let your ideas flow as organically as possible without trying to frame them in any particular way. Since no one is seeing, evaluating, or judging this, your complete, bare, naked, unfiltered honesty is *required*—no sugar coating, no buffering, no bullshit.

Question #1: Who are YOU on the day before you retire?
This question goes right to the heart of your identity and how you see yourself. I also want you to explore the idea of your emotional

---

3 Pam. A. Mueller and Daniel M. Oppenheimer, "The Pen is Mightier Than the Keyboard." *Psychological Science*, 25(6), 2014, 1159–1168.

4 Audry L.H. Vander Meer and Frederikus R. Van der Weel, "Only Three Fingers Write, but the Whole Brain Works: A High-Density EEG Study Showing Advantages of Drawing Over Typing for Learning." *Frontiers in Psychology*, 8, 2017, 706.

EXERCISE #1

Who Are You and What Do You Really Want Out of Retirement?

Who are YOU on the day before you retire?

_____

_____

_____

_____

_____

_____

Who are YOU on the day after?

_____

_____

_____

_____

_____

What do you want out of your next chapter?

_____

_____

_____

_____

_____

state, how you're feeling, and where those feelings reside (i.e., the pit of your stomach, your chest, etc.).

Question #2: Who are YOU on the day after?

The day after, your first day of your new life, can be a jumble of feelings and thoughts. Try to find the right words to fully describe where you are intellectually and emotionally. But take note, there's liable to be some deep feelings. Let it flow; no one is reading your words or sitting in judgment (unless you're already in "beat yourself up" mode. If you haven't yet experienced your "day after" yet, use your imagination to conjure an image that is true for you.

Question #3: What do you want out of your next chapter?

With all your being, capture the thoughts and feelings of what lies ahead. Don't sugarcoat it, and don't be afraid to be bold. It might change—in fact, it probably will—so don't worry about making it perfect.

This exercise is meant to "take your temperature" so that you may see what you're thinking is now. Don't worry, I don't expect you to have anything figured out yet. You will by the time you finish this book. But right now, notice your thoughts in their real and raw form. The nuances will come as you develop the self-awareness that will serve as your road map.

As I have mentioned before, we are going to leverage your lifetime of experience meeting challenges to help you move through this transition with strength and joy. OK, you might not be feeling the joy right at this moment—but you will, at the very least, feel competent to go forward with more confidence. Now that the pump is primed, I'm going to take you through another exercise. This one is a visualization. Don't groan! I'm not going to place you in a garden in the middle of the woods or in a mist-filled oasis. But I do want you to follow these instructions carefully.

Over the course of your career, you've had many "first" days. Whether it was a new job, marriage, divorce, becoming a parent, getting a promotion to new duties, becoming a coach for your kid's soccer team, or swinging a golf club for the first time, you have been constantly presented with new challenges and opportunities in which to become more than you were before. In this visualization, we're going to return to one of your biggest first days, that long ago day when you showed up at your *real* (think career) job for the very first time. Here are your instructions.

Be where you won't be disturbed.

Keep both feet on the floor.

Take five or six deep, calming breaths.

Ready?

* * *

Imagine it's your first day of work (post-education). Remember how you felt walking in the door, what you wore, what you thought about, who you interacted with. What were your expectations? What were your fears? Who showed you around? What was expected of you? Bring to mind everything you can remember from that day, including how you felt leaving the office at the end of the day.

Now, write your experience from beginning to end. Leave nothing out. Make the day real and raw. Stay in your memory without evaluation, and especially without self-judgment—just the emotions and images of your memory. Write it as if you were creating a screenplay for the movie of your life. Climb into your memories. Relive that day in vivid detail.

When you've completed the visualization and gotten it all down on paper, take a break. After you've had a chance to clear

VISUALIZATION #1

Your First Day of Work in the *Real* World

Who were you on your first day of work?

_____

_____

_____

_____

_____

_____

_____

_____

_____

What were your expectations?

_____

_____

_____

_____

_____

_____

_____

_____

_____

VISUALIZATION #1 (continued)

How did it turn out?

_____

_____

_____

_____

_____

_____

_____

_____

_____

What were your expectations?

_____

_____

_____

_____

_____

_____

_____

_____

_____

your head, read your recollection of the day. Highlight the words that best depict your emotional state at the time.

Were you fearful? Excited? Did you have positive expectancy? Did you see this as the beginning you'd imagined? What did you expect from yourself on day one? Did you see this day as the beginning of something meaningful and exciting? Anything else stand out? Now look at your answers from Exercise #1. Can you see any parallels or differences?

I have noticed that when working with men, their recollections are vivid, right down to the details of their desks, phones, and even the smell of their surroundings. One individual could even recount the taste of the coffee from the machine and how he became a black coffee drinker because he was too shy to ask about the location of the milk. Our memories can be our greatest ally in understanding who we are and how we became that way.

By way of example, I still recall with clarity, decades later, so many details of my first day at work:

July 12, 1976: I beat the sunrise by a good 30 minutes as my eyes flashed open before 5 a.m. I probably logged about four hours of sleep. After all, it was the first day of my professional life. I didn't think about all the work that went into getting my degree in accounting, nor did I think about the reasons for seeking that degree.

My morning routine was punctuated by the most careful shave of my life; making sure that no errant whiskers or stubble remained on my 21-year-old face. Staring into my closet, I had a choice of two suits, one gray and one brown; polyester both. Grabbing the gray one, a white starched shirt, a red-and-gray-patterned tie, and black socks and shoes, I began dressing, only to realize that I hadn't put on any deodorant. Not good . . . I was sweating already.

The office was a 10-minute drive; I was told to report at 9 a.m. I was dressed and ready by 5:36, in time to watch the sunrise. I would that day, I realized, witness two risings. I made a coffee and then panicked because I was afraid that I'd spill some on my dress shirt. I got undressed.

Eventually, it was time to leave. It was 8 a.m. I arrived at my destination, empty briefcase at the ready, at 8:09. I sat in the parking lot, sweating. What was waiting beyond the elevator doors on the second floor was beyond my comprehension. I was a jumble of nerves and tried to calm myself by taking deep breaths. Who would I be meeting? What would I be doing? Who would guide me? How will I know if I'm doing OK? The questions flooded my mind.

8:45 a.m.: Better to be early, I headed for the building entrance and entered the elevator. Three other men joined me. They were talking and didn't give me a second look, which was OK with me because I didn't think I could get a word out of my constricted throat. The doors opened, I allowed them to exit first. I watched them disappear through the inner door. I walked up to the window to an empty desk, so I took a seat in the spacious waiting room.

8:57 a.m.: "Can I help you?" a voice rang out from the open window at the receptionist's desk.

I squeaked out my name and that I was a new employee. "OK, sit tight, someone will be with you shortly."

9:10 a.m.: The door opened to reveal a middle-aged woman, with short, dark hair, olive skin, and plenty of gold necklaces standing in front of me. She introduced herself as Patty Pirillo, the office manager. I awkwardly shook her hand, hoping mine wasn't dripping wet. She took me through the office, introducing me to other accountants and staff as we went—none of their names stuck. She walked me through the kitchen where the coffee was and told me I was welcome to help myself whenever I wanted, showing neither where the cups were or anything else. The refrigerator, she said, was for anyone who brought in food, but I had to be sure to mark my name on it. She showed me to a cubicle and told me to wait there; someone would be with me shortly to get me started. She disappeared.

I sat at this desk, with a small electric adding machine on the left, a shelf for books, several drawers on the bottom right and a drawer in the middle. I explored the contents, finding errant paper clips, a few rubber bands, empty gum wrappers, and some clips that I would later discover were for binding work papers into folders.

9:45 a.m.: A young accountant entered my space and introduced himself as Ron. I shook his hand briskly. He dumped a ponderously large red rope folder on my desk and pulled out a file. He instructed me to begin to familiarize myself with the job and to "foot and crossfoot" several spreadsheets. I could feel my heart beating in my ears. He asked if there was anything I needed. My mind was racing. "Pencils? Erasers? The men's room?"

Your Values Are Signposts

As you reorient your thinking to what it means to evolve into retirement, we need to start with a clear understanding of values.

By starting our investigation with your memories of your "firsts," you can see yourself in the initial stages of "becoming" who you are today. With a firm understanding of this genesis, we can then turn our attention to gaining a clear understanding of the values that are the centerpiece of your character. Our values, which we begin to develop by listening to the messages we hear from our families, go through a process of acceptance or rejection, as we experience life through each developmental stage. Can you recall the values you held on your first day?

My father was a hard worker. He never talked about it; he was just constantly in motion, working. Whether as a teacher, a musician, a tutor, or attending to all the household jobs like gardener, plumber, carpenter, electrician, and painter, he worked *hard*! So, it isn't a surprise that with all that "active" modeling, I went into every job knowing I could and would outwork anyone. It was part of my values. As I walked into the office of the first CPA firm that hired me after graduation, I was always first in, last out (there's a pun in there for any accountants out there).

During my career as a financial life planner, the question of values was the centerpiece of all the planning work I did with my clients. I've held hundreds of conversations with clients, exploring what they valued to create a plan that reflected those values. I've had clients who've told me that they didn't care how much their children's college costs would be; they would happily pay (even through professional school). And I've had others who said they would be willing to contribute a specific amount to their kid's education, but demanded that the child had skin in the game. Still others told me that their kids would have figured it out for themselves. None of their answers were wrong; they reflected *their* values.

The beautiful thing about values is that they belong to you. You get to choose how you live based on those values. I devoted a lot of time to creating a list of what I really valued. As mentioned in Chapter 2, my core values are:

- My family
- Health
- My friends and relationships
- Helping others
- Learning new things

- ✕ Creativity
- ✕ Living joyfully

When confronted with a new opportunity, the first thing I ask myself is whether it aligns with my values. If it doesn't, I'm out. Quick story:

A few years ago, I was asked to play with a local community band. Remember, I am back playing trumpet after a 50-year hiatus, so I was very excited to play. I went to the first rehearsal with the group and found the people unfriendly. I also didn't love the music selected. I felt torn and considered whether to continue, noting that as an introvert, my discomfort might have been entirely my own. So, I went back to a second rehearsal. I felt the same. Being a firm believer in "finish what you start," I really felt conflicted. But I also knew that it was *not* joyful for me, and therefore conflicted with one of my values. So I handed my folder back to the conductor and gracefully exited. You either live your values, or you don't.

As you grow into your next chapter, it's time to think about what you value and why. Here is an offering of common values for you to consider:

Achievement, Authenticity, Balance, Community, Compassion, Creativity, Fairness, Family, Growth, Generosity, Health, Integrity, Legacy, Order, Tranquility, Learning, Security, Spirituality, Wisdom, Curiosity, Courage, Flexibility, Resilience, Gratitude, Humility, Loyalty, Patience . . . .

Feel free to add more.

Here is a worksheet that includes a more comprehensive list for you to choose your top values. Take note that you must know *why* these are so important to you. Create a list of three to five

EXERCISE #2

Create Your List of Values

Accountability	Equality	Justice	Self-discipline
Achievement	Ethics	Kindness	Self-expression
Adaptability	Excellence	Knowledge	Self-respect
Adventure	Fairness	Leadership	Serenity
Altruism	Faith	Learning	Service
Ambition	Family	Legacy	Simplicity
Authenticity	Financial stability	Leisure	Spirituality
Balance	Forgiveness	Love	Sportsmanship
Beauty	Freedom	Loyalty	Stewardship
Being the best	Friendship	Making a difference	Success
Belonging	Fun	Nature	Teamwork
Career	Future generations	Openness	Thrift
Caring	Generosity	Optimism	Time
Collaboration	Giving back	Order	Tradition
Commitment	Grace	Parenting	Travel
Community	Gratitude	Patience	Trust
Compassion	Growth	Patriotism	Truth
Competence	Harmony	Peace	Understanding
Confidence	Health	Perseverance	Uniqueness
Connection	Home	Personal fulfillment	Usefulness
Contentment	Honesty	Power	Vision
Contribution	Hope	Pride	Vulnerability
Cooperation	Humility	Recognition	Wealth
Courage	Humor	Reliability	Well-being
Creativity	Inclusion	Resourcefulness	Wholeheartedness
Curiosity	Independence	Respect	Wisdom
Dignity	Initiative	Responsibility	Willingness to learn
Diversity	Integrity	Risk-taking	
Environment	Intuition	Safety	
Efficiency	Job security	Security	

Write your own: Notes:

_____   _____

_____   _____

_____   _____

_____   _____

_____   _____

Download the full-size version of this worksheet from
https://michaelfkay.com/downloads/ • password: MYCHAPTERX

values that become the signposts for who you are and how you choose to live. Once you have your list, answer the why question. *Why* are these your values?

Once you have your three to five values figured out, we can begin to move forward—but with a very important caveat. You *might* change your mind about what you value as life and experiences unfold. Guess what? That's OK. This is your plan, your life, and your legacy. It's your responsibility to build it according to what you value most!

Here's a great exercise to try now that might inform or test what you think your most significant values are. It's one of the "Kinder Questions." George Kinder, who is credited as the founder of the financial life planning movement, developed three questions that become increasingly relevant to the core issues. While all three questions are important, we're going to focus on the third. Ready? The key to this exercise is, again, to be in a place where it's quiet and you can contemplate and write without interruption. In other words, *turn your phone off* and get your pen and paper ready.

$$\times \quad \times \quad \times$$

Imagine you are in the doctor's office. The doctor looks up from your file and tells you that you have 24 hours to live. Give yourself adequate time to allow this thought to sink in. Make it real! Ask yourself:

What did I miss?

Who did I not get to be?

What did I not get to do?

Write as much as you can draw out of yourself. Remember, no one is reading this. No one is judging you. This is for you to look deeply and fully into the mirror of your soul and grapple with

VISUALIZATION #2

You Have One Day to Live

What did I miss?

_____

_____

_____

_____

_____

_____

Who did I not get to be?

_____

_____

_____

_____

_____

_____

What did I not get to do?

_____

_____

_____

_____

_____

_____

_____

your life, your past, and your future. Caution: this exercise can sometimes bring to the surface powerful emotions, so be ready.

After you've completed this exercise, I suggest you give yourself time and space to ease out of the experience. Spend some time in nature, take a walk, and avoid external stimuli as much as possible. Time in nature is associated with lower cortisol levels,[5] calming the sympathetic nervous system, and promoting a sense of peace. After this exercise, it's a great antidote.

What you discovered here can be used as a foundation for building a life of meaning and purpose. For example, I worked with a client who was a lifelong committed workaholic. He was rarely present for his children's events, like soccer and baseball. He was an executive for a Fortune 50 company, working enormous hours, traveling globally, and feeling exhausted when he was home. He completed the exercise in my office and literally sat in my conference room in tears. His work life was a highlight reel of success, but the cost was tremendous. He recognized that he couldn't replace the missed time with his children, but he could dedicate his life in retirement to repairing the relationship and spending quality time with them and his grandchildren. One of his first acts was to gather his three children and apologize to them for what he had missed. He didn't get to be a "dad" while they were young. He recognized that he missed so much by sacrificing time together for financial and career success. When we worked on his list of values, one of the first values was family, along with the actions he could take to be a caring and doting grandfather.

What did you learn about yourself from the "one day to live" visualization? How can you use that knowledge to add to the formula of creating a meaningful, purposeful, and joyful life? You

---

5 Myron F. Hunter, B.W. Gillespie, and S.Y.P. Chen. "Urban nature experiences reduce stress in the context of daily life baded on salivary biomarkers." *Frontiers in Psychology*, 2019. 10:722. doi:10.3389/fpsyg.2019.00722

might have regrets, deep and hurtful ones that burn your insides. But I will tell you this right now as clearly as possible: living in regret is like landing on "Go to Jail" in Monopoly. Not only is it a clear path to misery, but it is also directly linked to increased depression, anxiety, chronic stress, and emotional fatigue. No one needs that, especially you, as you embark upon this magical time in your life where fulfillment and joy await.

One more thing about regret: did you know it can be powerfully transformational? It can add to personal development, wisdom, greater resilience, empathy, and clarity of values. There is substantial research on regret and how to work through it to achieve positive outcomes. Without getting into the weeds, the process involves six steps:

1. Name it: Be specific about regret—what was lost, what value it violated.
2. Accept imperfection: Recognize that mistakes are all a part of the human experience.
3. Reframe: What did you learn? How have you changed?
4. Make amends: If possible, take steps to repair or acknowledge the damage done.
5. Act forward: Use regret as a fuel for better choices.
6. Seek professional support: This one's huge. Getting help before it becomes a festering wound is critical.

Time to Celebrate and Rest

Here we are. You've done great work, hard work, to look back on your past experiences and identify the values that light the fire in your belly. Align your values to help craft and guide how you live your life going forward. What are the activities and involvements that resonate with those values? If you value creativity, why would you spend your life doing things (beyond the necessities) that are not creative? If you value learning, what can you do to promote it? You get the picture. You are the gatekeeper of your values and actions.

With the exercises in this chapter, you've seen yourself through your memories and the values you walked into your professional life with. Hopefully, you've noticed how beginnings are filled with anxiety, fear, excitement, and uncertainty, and that experience teaches us that change and growth are a natural progression. This process of growth is a part of how we develop our values. Now that you know what your values are, no more deflecting time and attention to things that are counter to who you are and to what makes you, well, you!

In the next chapter, I'll uncover the tools you already possess to successfully navigate from your structured, comfortable work life to your Chapter X.

A VIEW FROM CHAPTER

"All That Glitters" by Bruce Meisterman

One of the things I take away from Chapter X is that the concerns, issues, and fears are universal. Relevancy, vitality, and identity appear to be at stake. Of course, we know better, but they do exist, and how we deal with them is likely the larger issue. There is no one-size-fits-all solution.

For some of us, the need for community is greater than for others. Some of us may welcome the privacy and solitude that retirement provides us. Or a combination of the two. How does one measure a successful retirement? And does what we learned in our previous iteration apply to our current version of ourselves?

Is it possible to measure wisdom through the lens of experience? Some of what we may have learned in business doesn't work in retirement. Do the lessons we learned count for anything? In my case, the hard knowledge I gained at work no longer applies. But the soft skills, people, and behavior do. That may count as wisdom.

I have helped others by setting examples, assisting them in achieving their goals, or demonstrating how to grow a business. That, frankly, is a good measure of success, theirs as well as mine.

Values? That depends on who you speak with. I attended a seminar in Toronto some years ago with a group of people whose values and beliefs were similar to mine, but their interest in my work changed that. They were confounded how I could do what I did and still profess to hold the same values as they did. I was in marketing and media, and they perceived that as an evil enterprise, hawking products and services no one needed. Try as I did, I could not convince them of the value of that work. My work was not seen as valuable. Ask my clients and they would disagree. So would my family. Here's the fly in that ointment: Would I have done the same work if another alternative were available? Probably not. Were my values compromised? I still can't answer that.

Ah, success. See the first sentence of the last paragraph. Over the past weekend, my wife and I attended a regional production of *A Bronx Tale*, a story based on the play by Chazz Palminteri. Was it Broadway quality? Of course not. Were the actors good? Was it a success? Gauging from the audience response, the answer would be yes. If this were a tryout for Broadway, would any of the participants be selected? Not likely. But on this level, it succeeded. This is where it gets personal and a struggle to reconcile.

If my book doesn't get picked up by a publisher and I have to self-publish it, is it a success? Is it a failure? Will I make it to "Broadway" or not? If not, can I be content with the alternative? In business, there were parameters in which our success could be measured. By that criterion, yes, I was very successful, though the accompanying stress and toll it took were still being paid. Is the accomplishment of completing the book and being relegated to a regional production enough? At least the stress level is way down. Stay tuned.

CHAPTER 5

Grab Your Tools

> "Ability is what you're capable of doing.
> Motivation determines what you do. Attitude
> determines how well you do it."
> —Lou Holtz, former Notre Dame head football coach

After all those decades of building your skills, refining your abilities, growing, climbing the ladder of success, and single-mindedly focused on your career, you're about to be cut loose from everything you know ... well, sort of. We've talked about the fact that you will go from structure to no structure, from accountability to none, from mastery to, once again, novice. Yes, you are, or soon will be, a novice at retirement. Feels scary, right? Take a breath, it will be OK. Trust me. You have the tools. You might need to see it, understand it, and maybe do a little reframing. In the last chapters, you've begun the exciting task of examining your perceptions and identity, and of connecting your real-life experiences (such as your first day of work) to your values. You also did an end-of-life reflection that centered on regret (a state that we wish to avoid at all costs, except as a learning tool).

Let's get something clear. You've gone from novice to mastery over and over and over again throughout your life. This is just one more revolution in your evolution. Through each step, each phase, you've accumulated experience and honed your abilities. And you've developed a set of tools that make you capable of adapting to change. Here are some of the main ones:

- Problem-solving
- Learning
- Flexibility
- Resilience
- Creativity
- Communicating with others
- Understanding purposeful action

Let's face it, you've been solving problems since your diaper was wet. We are problem-solving machines at heart. The problem before you now is, how do you redirect your thinking from work challenges to life challenges that are focused on your values? And how does that relate to moving your goals forward? If you've ever driven a stick shift car, you know the feeling of downshifting to a lower gear—the unpleasant jolt from a nice, smooth fifth to a laborious second, especially when climbing a steep hill or hitting a patch of snow. Sometimes big life transitions can feel the same way, bumpy and a bit distressing. But you have plenty of experience to know that things do smooth out once you find your gear and resume cruising toward your destination. After all, if you think back to the first day of work exercise, Day 2 was probably slightly less stressful than Day 1, and by the end of the first month, there was, most likely, greater comfort.

Let's again refer back to your first day of work exercise. Think about what problems you solved on Day 1. There may have been several! Maybe it was just figuring out how to get to the office or finding out where they kept the coffee cups. You'll be using the worksheets that follow to help you recover stories and experiences from your life that demonstrate your capabilities. I want you to know, right down to your marrow, that you have what it takes to get through this challenging transition successfully.

This next exercise is rather detailed and lengthy, so make sure you're well rested, focused, and ready. You might need to take a break in between sections, which is all good. I suggest that before you begin or after a break, you get yourself grounded with your feet on the floor and a few deep breaths. During my interaction with men after they've tackled this exercise, I've seen their eyes light up with recognition. It becomes apparent through their life experiences that the task of working through this change becomes less daunting and more exciting. Go for it! (Exercise sheets begin on the next page.)

Problem-Solving

Starting at the top, think about an example from your life and/or career where you successfully demonstrated PROBLEM-SOLVING.

I am sure you can recall countless instances of your problem-solving ability. After all, you've been walking the planet for some time now and have accumulated lots of opportunities to refine your abilities. Locate in your mind an example of a real brain buster. Think of an instance where you really had to dig deeply to develop a pathway forward.

When I reflect on challenging problems in my own life, I always remember a situation with a client who had a rather difficult personality. I really loved this guy. He was creative, strong, and forward-thinking. The problem was that he was a pain in the ass when he decided he knew better in areas clearly outside the scope of his knowledge and experience. I wrestled with how to deal with someone who was volatile, yet incredibly talented. He triggered me. I knew I could fire him as a client, but I was

EXERCISE #3

Uncovering the Tools That You Already Have

What was an example, in your life and/or career, where you successfully demonstrated PROBLEM SOLVING?

_____

_____

_____

_____

_____

What was an example, in your life and/or career, where you successfully demonstrated LEARNING?

_____

_____

_____

_____

_____

What was an example, in your life and/or career, where you successfully demonstrated RESILIENCE?

_____

_____

_____

_____

_____

_____

EXERCISE #3 (continued)

What was an example, in your life and/or career, where you successfully demonstrated CREATIVITY?

_____

_____

_____

_____

_____

What was an example, in your life and/or career, where you successfully demonstrated COMMUNICATION WITH OTHERS?

_____

_____

_____

_____

What was an example, in your life and/or career, where you successfully demonstrated FLEXIBILTY?

_____

_____

_____

_____

EXERCISE #3 (continued)

What was an example, in your life and/or career, where you successfully demonstrated UNDERSTANDING PURPOSEFUL ACTION?

_____

_____

_____

_____

_____

_____

_____

_____

What are some OTHER SKILLS that served you in the past that were connected to your success?

_____

_____

_____

_____

_____

_____

_____

_____

committed to his success. It took me a while to figure out how to approach the situation without being triggered and to engage with him differently so that we could work together. I'm glad I put in the effort because, in time, we came to respect each other, and, most importantly, I was able to help him achieve his goals.

Let me quickly share a problem-solving tip that's helped me a great deal. Sometimes the first step is merely naming or identifying the problem. Why? Because it puts you on the right track and prevents you from "solving" the wrong problem!

In your next phase of life, after you're no longer your job or title, you will need to problem-solve things like filling your time with activities that bring you joy, creating new or continuing to support existing relationships, dealing with medical challenges, and navigating Medicare and Social Security. It's a lot! Maybe you're starting to think about just how "easy" life has been until now?

Learning

The next tool is that of LEARNING. Just like problem-solving, we are learning from infancy. While not intentional, we cried when we were hungry, and, lo and behold, sustenance appeared. *That* is learning, my friend. Consider each step in your journey from novice to mastery, all the stages you've been through, all the learning that occurred (it's a prodigious amount, when you really think about it!). Now multiply that by the number of times you started back at novice, only to move forward once again toward mastery.

Coming from a family of professional musicians, I was naturally drawn to music. My uncle, an incredibly talented and renowned trombonist, suggested I learn trumpet. After rudimentary instruction from the school's music teacher, my mother found a teacher for me to continue my studies. He was a member of the New York Philharmonic and a demanding and emotional teacher.

OK, let me rephrase that—he broke me, literally, to tears every week. He had two students, one who was in the Juilliard School of Music, and me, a freshman in high school. He was brutally demanding. But guess what? I learned a lot.

When I was 18, I heard a recording of trumpeter Jon Faddis, who was also 18 and a protégé of the iconic Dizzy Gillespie. His ability made it clear that I was nowhere near on the same planet of ability. The difference was so astounding, so profound, that I decided not to pursue a music career (to my parents' relief). I put the horn in the case and put it away. That is learning.

We are born to learn, to grow, to experience. The idea that retirement is the cessation of learning and growth is, to say the least, absurd. Retirement isn't about sitting on the front porch waiting to die. Retirement is about channeling all you know, all you've done, all your experiences as a propellant into this chapter of life with energy, enthusiasm, and positive expectations. It's just different from what you've been doing since you started working in that there's no financial remuneration, no job title, no organization to which you're beholden.

Let's go back to the worksheet and complete the section on LEARNING. Write about an example from your life and/or career where you successfully demonstrated your learning ability. I'm sure you can come up with thousands of "a-ha" moments of learning. Remember, we learn from curiosity and from new and different situations and circumstances in which we find ourselves.

I can't help but share another learning story. I met my wife in my sophomore year of college. She actually approached me with the intention of fixing me up with her girlfriend, but we hit it off at our first meeting. Being a bit of a smartass, I picked up on her Boston accent and mimicked her when I heard her say certain words. She didn't like it, and I could see the look of, not disgust, exactly, but let's just say she didn't find the humor in it. I quickly learned that if I wanted to pursue a relationship, continuing on that track wasn't going to cut it. That, too, is learning, my friend.

Can you see the point of connecting what you already know, what you've done over and over and over again throughout your life, to this new chapter? To many people, retirement feels empty, devoid of meaning and purpose. It's unnavigable to them, being so completely new and out of touch with their experience that moving forward seems impossible. That's not you. Let's move forward.

Resilience

The next stop on the journey is RESILIENCE. Do you see yourself as resilient? This is often a fun topic in my Chapter X interactions. Why? Because we all have our war stories. We've all had to grit our teeth and tough it out.

What about you? How many times have you been knocked down and gotten up again? Think about your toddler-self. You got up, took a step or two, and fell. You didn't stay down, did you? When you were a bit older, you fell off your bike and got back on. You were resilient! The Chapter X version of you also needs to be resilient because, as you know, aging isn't pretty, even for the healthiest of us.

I started my professional career as an accountant, working in small and medium-sized CPA firms. I did everything from mom-and-pop businesses to SEC audits. I did bankruptcy cases and tax preparation. I worked on tax shelters and divorce cases. I did physical inventories of chicken-processing plants and chemical companies. I traveled across the country working on clients' accounts. I also started my own small practice in my first year, in which I continued my breakneck maniacal style of working. I worked for amiable partners and some who were unreasonable assholes. But I had a family to support and a career to build, and I had to learn how to deal with all sorts of personalities and behaviors.

After nearly 10 years, I "cashed in" my CPA license for a position with a friend in the financial services industry. I knew nothing about insurance, planning, and investments, but I loved the idea of being future-thinking, rather than dealing with the past. I quickly learned the ins and outs of the business, also realizing that I pretty much suck at selling. I had some great years and some miserable years. But each defeat was just the nudge to learn, change, and create what needed to happen next. The pressure was intense, and I found myself in financial and emotional misery. I needed to move into alignment with who I was and with what felt right for me. I decided to move out of the office and open my own space. I began to build a practice that reflected my values and allowed me to focus on growing a sustainable client base with recurrent income, not commissions.

I built my firm from that idea and eventually created a fee-only multi-advisor firm focused on advice, without regard to product. I needed every resilient molecule in my body to transform from a stable CPA to a failed salesperson and then to a successful entrepreneur and advisor.

My guess is, you've been knocked around, too—time to go to the worksheet and complete the resilience section. Your Chapter X will be filled with opportunities to exercise your resilient muscle. The bad news is that it's mostly unfamiliar territory. The good news is that you've been in unfamiliar territory many times before and found your bearings. Take a minute to capture the memory of times when you've been in new situations that challenged you, brought you to failure, and how you bounced back. I can't say it enough: you've done it all, time and time and time again. This situation feels different because, well, it is. But each time in the past, it was different too. The common thread is the resilience muscle that you've developed throughout your lifetime. And each time, it was the tools in your repertoire that helped you through.

Creativity

I love to talk about CREATIVITY. Mostly because I hear so many people tell me that they aren't creative, and I remain skeptical and nonbelieving. I don't care about your imagined belief. We all possess creativity in some ways, and I guarantee that if you think about it, you will see it in yourself. There are very few great artists, musicians, writers, sculptors, or dancers. But so what? I imagine you have creatively dealt with a situation or two that required a level or two of imagination beyond the mundane.

One of the wondrous aspects of Chapter X is the freedom to explore creativity without expectation, without a demanding client or boss to satisfy. But a note of caution: if your measurement for creativity is that anything you do must reach the level of genius and be acclaimed by the world as such, you're missing the point. The joy of creativity is that of personal exploration and expression. Your ability to be creative requires that you remove the goal of mastery, of superlative outcomes, of perfection. Maybe you expected only top performance from yourself throughout your work life, but as a creative human, you need to free yourself of the idea of mastery as you begin new explorations.

I had a client who was a top executive of a very large public company. When he retired, he got involved in his living community and played softball, and he also began to build furniture. He showed me pictures of what he created, and over the course of years, his work went from really nice to *spectacular*.

I met a potter at a street fair. I admit freely that I am a sucker for pottery mugs, still in a lifelong search for the perfect fit and feel. We started talking about his work and the sources for his creativity. Turns out he is a retired teacher who had never done pottery before but found it fun. His work is beautiful. Yes, I bought three.

It doesn't matter whether you write, paint, sculpt, play music, build furniture, or do anything that allows you to explore parts of you that have either been untapped or untouched—this is the time to turn the key in the lock.

During my life, I've done a lot of writing. I contributed to my high school and college papers. I wrote throughout my financial planning career, both books and articles. But I always had a draw to writing fiction. A friend suggested I attend a writer's conference and listen to the speakers and mix with writers from all over. It was a wonderful and affirming experience. I decided to start writing a short story. Drawing from an experience I had as an auditor, I wrote a story about an accountant who was thrust into the audit of a nursing home. The story took me on an unexpected journey. The story, titled "Just Another Lousy Tax Season," was published by a literary site, Half & One. This is an example of taking the thread of an idea and weaving it into something fun and different.

You can find at least one situation where you needed to think creatively to meet your goals or where you unexpectedly used your innate creativity. Grab your worksheet and write it out. What was an example in your life and/or career where you successfully demonstrated CREATIVITY?

Creativity is one of your key tools in Chapter X. It's expansive, covers a lot of territory, and is something you'll come back to time and again. Why? Because creativity is not just art or music or writing, it's using your mind in ways that require less linear and more outside-the-box thinking. I don't care if the apex of your creative life was in making an ashtray out of popsicle sticks; the ability to bring something from your heart, soul, and guts into reality is something we are born with. It's an inborn quality we should cherish and make full use of.

I watch my granddaughters in all their creative glory, joyfully coloring, pasting colored gems to a page, dancing, and making up games. It's pure joy. Don't you want some?

My friend, Bruce Meisterman, a member of the Chapter X community, has written several books since his retirement. I asked him to share some thoughts on the topic of creativity. Here are a few great ones he provided:

> "It's a way to communicate with others, the world, and oneself."
>
> "The spark of creativity need not dwell within— inspiration can come from anywhere and is often the most unlikely source. The light reflecting off a hubcap inspired my first fiction book. The twisted mind that I have went to a premise, 'What if all light disappeared and reappeared on its own accord?'"
>
> "At its simplest, creativity is another way of looking at something and saying, 'What if?' It taps into an awareness."

Can you look back and see creativity in your life? Can you look forward and imagine how creativity can play an essential role in joyful and meaningful acts? Let's pause a second: I want to make sure that there is clarity in the idea of meaningful acts. A meaningful act is meaningful to *you*. It doesn't mean or imply that it needs to reach into the next room, the next house, the next street. We are harsh judges of ourselves, and this needs to be tempered and tamed as you move into the next phase of life. If we hold onto the idea that only actions that have societal or global implications are important, then we are missing the point. More than that, we're dooming ourselves to frustration. Sure, it would be cool if we tripped over a cure for cancer or a workable solution to end hunger, but, come on, you gotta kiss reality somewhere near the mouth. It isn't selfish to find fulfillment and enjoyment in your actions and activities after a lifetime of work. Get it? If not, don't worry, I will remind you again . . . and again.

Communications

The next tool in your kit is COMMUNICATIONS, the ability to create understanding between people. We've learned to communicate our wants, needs, feelings, and beliefs from our earliest days. We've learned what works and what doesn't, and that the same modes and methods don't work the same for everyone. In Chapter X, we transition from a lifetime of being on a singular track (building a career, wealth, security) to a life where we're not the boss or employee. We're not in control of the fate of our work's mission. This means our channels of communication have changed—and this is a big factor, because many men aren't that great at communicating outside of the purview of work. Even so, we still have the essential skills, honed over decades, to share our thoughts and ideas with others. It's the same, only different.

In my years as a financial life planner, communication was the centerpiece of my professional life. I had interactions with clients, colleagues, and staff. It was a joy to be with the members of the firm, sharing stories, ideas, and experiences. We were a family, even to the extent of having our own Thanksgiving together, where everyone contributed a dish or bottle to the celebration. I wrote for various publications, wrote two books, and spoke at conferences as far away as Mumbai. Life was about the communication of ideas.

In Chapter X, that was gone in a blink. No more office Thanksgivings. No more consulting on client situations, no more sharing family issues (both celebrations and tragedies). It was an emotional loss. If I wanted to go out to lunch, I either had to wait for my phone to ring or reach out to others to make those social connections. What was once easy has now become challenging. I no longer had regular interactions with my once-close work family. I no longer had people popping their heads in to chat, ask questions, or share personal issues. In my Chapter X, I needed to move out of my comfort zone to create new relationships and actively support my old ones with satisfying and meaningful communications.

Quick story about reaching out, in this case, *way* out. One day, for no apparent reason, I was sitting outside at our getaway in the Berkshires, and the name of a childhood friend popped into my mind. His name is Marty Kanengiser, and we were good friends in elementary school until he went to a private school in junior high. I hadn't seen or heard from him since. But since his name arrived unexpectedly in my cranial inbox, I looked him up on LinkedIn. The P.S. to the story is that Marty was my first Chapter X podcast guest, and we now see each other (and together as couples) several times a year. He is valued in my heart, and reconnecting was really meaningful.

Head back to your worksheet and complete the question: What is an example, in your life and/or career, where you successfully demonstrated your skill and ability in communicating with others? I have no doubt you have a million examples, so write an example that clearly illustrates how you might have challenged your comfort zone to create meaningful communications with others. Then step back a moment and ask, "What am I learning from these exercises?" Are you seeing the glue that connects your life from early childhood, through your formative years, into and through your professional career, to the present? And all the ways in which you have the capacity to grow, learn, communicate, and show your resilience?

Flexibility

One of the tools we need to grasp is the idea of FLEXIBILITY. Indeed, you have demonstrated this wonderful cognitive ability to shift thoughts and actions quickly and seamlessly. You know, like heading to your destination, route in mind, when traffic has another idea and suddenly your mapped out trail needs to be rethought. Or better yet, working on a project that consumed your thoughts when suddenly something urgent occurs and you have to shift gears to focus on another matter entirely.

In Chapter X, "dry holes" happen. You start digging into a new project or plan when you hit a dead end. You can meet this "defeat" in two ways: you can feel bad about it and sulk and lean into disappointment, or you can engage your flexibility muscle to shift your attention to something more satisfying. If Plan A doesn't work, what's Plan B or C or D? You've had to deal with these many times during your career. If your ideas at work didn't pan out to your expectations, you didn't walk out and quit your job; you figured it out.

In my former life as a CPA, I did a lot of auditing work. It was intensely plan-focused and required a team that understood the goal and how to get there. Since I didn't work for a big firm, we were expected to go back to the office during tax season to do tax returns after a day of auditing. Auditing and tax work are about as similar as diamonds and cream cheese. But, hey, after a day of diamonds, I got to switch to a night of cream cheese. It was what needed to be done.

Speaking of flexibility, a friend of mine was working for a rather large corporation when a rather larger company swooped in and acquired his firm. Six months after the acquisition, he found himself without a position. When he saw the proverbial writing on the wall, he began digging into his network, looking for a new opportunity. He didn't sulk. He didn't whine or despair. He just figured out how to move forward.

I am confident that with a bit of thought, you can recall times when you needed to engage your flexibility muscle. Your worksheet beckons . . . . Write an example from your life and/or career where you demonstrated FLEXIBILITY. Make sure to cite an example (or two) that really shows you at your flexible best. Think about your mindset when you needed to be flexible and adapt, through no fault of your own, from thought to thought, action to action, idea to idea, to see things through and land on your feet.

If anything is certain, you will be faced with challenges during this next chapter unlike any you've probably been faced with before. Your ability to adapt, change, shift, and move with the current of circumstances will be the key to your happiness, and, in fact, survival. Your unwillingness or inability to change your thinking, your actions, and your mindset will undoubtedly lead to misery.

Purposeful Action

The last tool we're going to discuss in this chapter is PURPOSEFUL ACTION. Damn, I know you've got this one! Your entire adult life has been a symphony of purposeful action. You had a mission; you got it done. Well, my friend, life after work is just a continuation of purposeful action. Let me put it plainly, with an exclamation point at the end: you pick your purpose, whether it is playing with your grandkids, taking a nap when your body needs it, taking a walk, helping a friend, playing a round of golf, sitting on a nonprofit board, writing a book, learning a language, taking a course, painting a house, working in a garden, spending time with your spouse/partner—you get to choose!

In other words, the purpose that drove you during your career is not the right measuring device for the importance or meaning of what you do after your career has wrapped up. That's why getting caught up in your title, occupation, or profession as the yardstick for your sense of purpose is so dangerous and leads to disappointment, depression, and hanging an "I used to be" tag next to your name.

When I was a young teen and music began to surge in my brain, I determined that it was what was most important to me. It was my purpose. I decided that the student model Olds trumpet just wouldn't cut it. I had started working at a local butcher shop every day after school. My job was simple: clean, scrub, and make everything shiny and immaculate. My boss, Al Roth, was like a second father. He was an ex-Marine rifle instructor and cook. He explained that there was only one acceptable outcome: perfection in everything I did. If a job didn't meet his standards, I had to do it again until it passed his scrutiny.

I had been working and saving money to satisfy my music habit, but when I set my sights on a Silver Getzen Doc Severinsen model horn, I knew that I had to step up my game. Those horns were pricey! Three doors down from the butcher shop was the bagel store. I got to know the owner, Phil. He asked me if I wanted to work for him on the weekends when the butcher shop was closed. I jumped at the chance to make more money. I worked Saturday nights from 6 p.m. to midnight and Sunday mornings from 5:30 a.m. to 2 p.m. That's where I became known as the Butcher-Bagel Boy of West Orange. I had a purpose. I didn't mind the hours. I wanted that horn!

It seems simple enough at first thought. You need to conduct your life "on purpose" and not allow yourself to sit on the couch. Your purpose doesn't need to be grandiose or earth-changing. Anything you do that comes from a conscious decision is purposeful. It's as simple as that. Don't get me wrong, there may be days when you just need to do nothing, but that, too, can be purposeful.

I spoke to a friend who is retired. He was a very successful executive dealing with cutting-edge technology. He shared that his neighbor just retired and is committed to sitting on the couch watching CNN. I asked about the man and was told he was a prominent corporate attorney with a very big job. But now, all he does is watch the screen. I wonder, what happened to this once-driven man's sense of purpose? How can he be satisfied sitting on the sofa all day? How did he lose all sense of his direction and vision? What does he see as the purpose for his life going forward?

Yes, it's that time. Pick up your pen and worksheet and write an example, in your life and/or career, where you demonstrated PURPOSEFUL ACTION. I'm sure you can fill volumes just recalling everything you've accomplished through your purposeful actions. Even lottery winners have to "do something" to win.

Put Your Tools to Work!

Do you see all the tools you possess after a lifetime of experience? You've got your problem-solving ability, all the learning, the resilience, creativity, communications with others, flexibility, and purposeful actions that have filled your life since earliest childhood. You've basically devoted a lifetime to preparing for your life after work—you just didn't realize it. Chapter X may not look so scary when you learn how well equipped you are to handle it!

In the next chapter, I'll talk about some additional helpful tools that you might not be aware of, plus some others that might need your attention. We'll also talk about relationships and how they need to be considered in this next stage of life. Then I'll focus on a tool called "The Wheel of Life in Retirement," which you can use as an assessment for what's working and what needs your attention.

I don't want to end this chapter without noting that while we are rediscovering and honing our existing tools, we have other assets that we might not be thinking about. I'm talking about our loved ones, family members, close friends, and those who make up our community. Those who help us feel connected. If this is an area of concern for you, do not ignore it! Focus on it with ardor because having a team, a community, or a tribe is essential for living a fulfilling post-career life.

But for now, give yourself a big hug or get one from someone you love for all the great work you've done so far! Time for a break.

A VIEW FROM CHAPTER

"My Unretirement" by Richard Eisenberg

I was lucky to spend a 40+ year career as a personal finance writer and editor at places like *Money* magazine, CBS MoneyWatch, *USA Today*, and, ultimately PBS's Next Avenue (a website for people 50+). But in 2022, when I hit 65 and marked my 10th anniversary at Next Avenue, I began having a nagging feeling.

I felt it was time to step away from my job as Next Avenue's Managing Editor to begin my next chapter of life: unretirement.

My plan, somewhat vague at the time, was to give myself the opportunity to do things I couldn't (or *thought* I couldn't) while holding down a full-time job, such as volunteering, mentoring, freelancing, traveling with my wife, visiting our grown sons and their wives across the country in Los Angeles, and upping my schedule recording the "Friends Talk Money" personal finance podcast I co-host.

I also wanted to try doing *new* things, such as voiceover work, and stop doing things like attending Next Avenue staff meetings and managing invoices.

After consulting with my wife and our financial advisor, I gulped and told my Next Avenue boss my plans to resign in three months. Gratefully, I learned I'd be able to freelance for the site, and I've been doing so for more than three years now.

The transition to unretirement has felt freeing and joyful. In addition to freelancing, I have spent three summers running an NYU digital media program for young adults and teaching an NYU virtual Master Class in unretirement for older ones. I've found sharing my expertise, knowledge, and maybe a little wisdom to be extremely rewarding.

Unretirement has also been a little unmooring. While I've loved the extra time, deciding how (and how much) to fill it up has sometimes felt challenging. It's quite a shift going from a planned, daily schedule to a blank calendar.

I've learned that finding outlets where I can freelance and earn income takes time and effort, too. In today's mercurial world of journalism, guarantees of steady work have grown fewer. Soon after beginning my unretirement, I started writing regularly about Medicare for Fortune.com, but that came to an end in 2025 when the outlet lost its freelance budget.

Still, I have no major financial complaints. I'm lucky to have two pensions from former jobs, a chunk of money in rollover 401(k)s, Social Security, a small amount of freelance income each month, Medicare, and both Medigap and long-term care policies. But I confess to missing a steady paycheck.

All in all, I'd call my unretirement a success by my metrics. I'm living life according to my values, learning new things, helping others, and reveling in newfound time with my wife, our family, and now a granddaughter.

CHAPTER 6

Three Tools You May Not Know You Have, But Need: Groundedness, Growth Mindset, Generativity

> "We make a living by what we get.
> We make a life by what we give."
> —*Winston Churchill, British statesman*

In our last chapter, you did an amazing amount of work. You dug deeply into your core memories for demonstrable examples of the valuable, productive, and meaningful tools you possess. It's funny, on first thought, that you might not have realized how expansive your skills in problem-solving, learning, flexibility, resilience, creativity, communications, and understanding purposeful action really are. These abilities are a part of us that we don't see when we look in the mirror; we take them, by and large, for granted. But they are always ready to be called upon, and, boy, have they seen you through some challenges in your life.

In this chapter, we will examine three tools that are the bedrock of developing wisdom and living a life of meaning. The three are groundedness, growth mindset, and generativity. They are even more "under the radar" than the tools in the last chapter, but they are always there, helping to gently guide you through the decisions you make and the actions you take.

While these three tools are probably already in your toolbox, they may not seem relevant in the context of life after career. I'll start with groundedness, simply because it's essential to have your feet on the floor and your head in the game.

Groundedness

I've mentioned previously that aging is not for the faint of heart; the challenges are significant. Not only are you dealing with the issues I've pointed to earlier (loss of identity, routine, social structure, purpose, etc.), but also with the effects on your brain and body from living this long. Being grounded in the reality of the moment is important. In other words, taking an inventory of where you are and what's going well and what's not, what needs attention, and what is humming along just fine. Your deep awareness of your reality is the baseline from which you make decisions in terms of where you need to put your attention.

There is an assessment tool I use called The Wheel of Life in Retirement. It was developed by Money Quotient, the company responsible for my financial life planning training, to whom I owe a lifetime of gratitude. The tool is on the following page.

As you can see, the wheel displays nine categories for you to assess. Intellectual Engagement, Productive Pursuits, Leisure/Recreation, Healthcare & Physical Fitness, Close Relationships, Community & Social Relationships, Home & Location, Personal Growth, Financial Well-Being. Follow the instructions above the wheel, but don't make this too complicated. If it's a 10, it's a 10; if it's a 2, it's a 2. Note: If you're not doing anything in a category and that's precisely what you want right now, it's a 10.

EXERCISE #4

The Wheel of Life in Retirement

Directions: This exercise will help you to assess your growth and development in each facet of life in retirement. It will also help you to evaluate the degree of balance and level of life satisfaction you are now experiencing.

Step #1: Place a dot on each spoke that indicates your level of satisfaction in that particular facet of life. Use a scale of 0 to 10, with 0 at the hub and 10 at the rim. A 0 indicates no satisfaction and a 10 indicates the highest degree of satisfaction.

Step #2: Now draw a line to connect the dots and create your life wheel.

Step #3: Evaluate your wheel. Is your life wheel round or does it show flat spots? Is it deflated or is it full? What does this exercise tell you about your life? Is your life balanced? Are there areas of your life that need attention? In what facets would you like to experience more satisfaction?

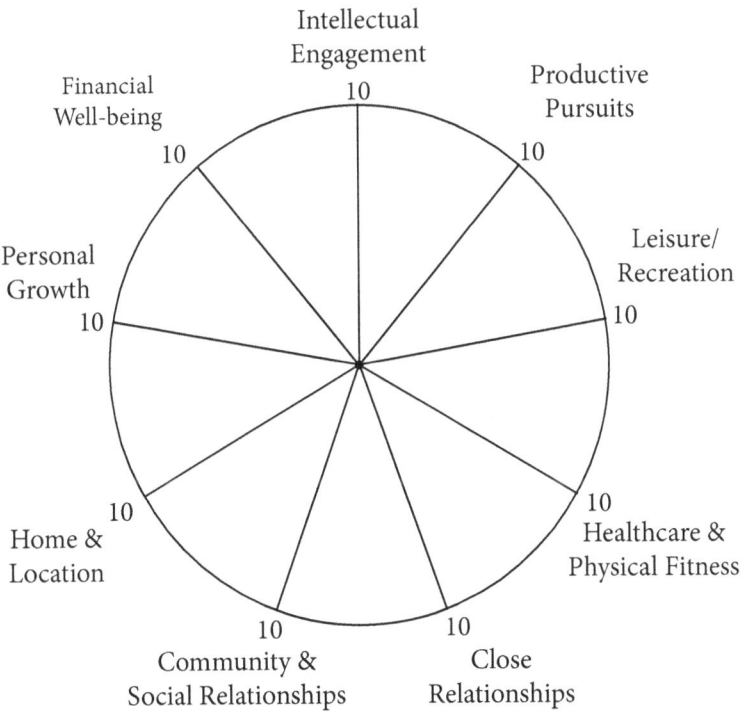

Download the full-size version of this worksheet from
https://michaelfkay.com/downloads/ • password: MYCHAPTERX

After you've placed the dots on each spoke and connected them to see your wheel, stand back and take it in. This picture is a snapshot of how you feel *today*. It's not permanent! Personally, I fill this out several times a year to see what's changed, in either direction. It also shows me where I wish to put my energies.

I'm going to share a vivid example of just how valuable this tool is and what a good job it does in marking change (for better or worse). Following is my Wheel of Retirement from January 10, 2021, when I retired from my career and entered Chapter X. As you can see, I gave myself high marks all around. I was feeling pretty good about my life.

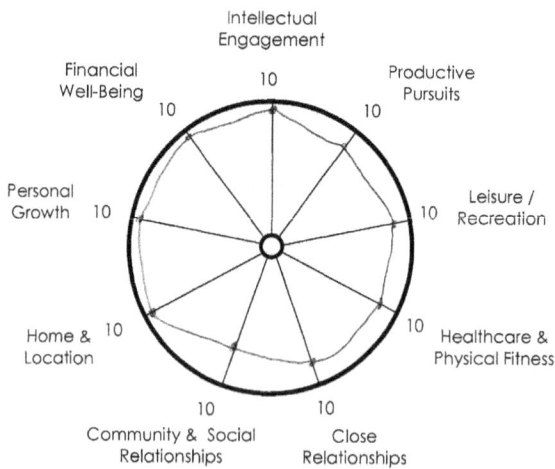

Four months later, I crashed. Remember me talking about this earlier in the book—my feeling high as a kite to begin with, but soon smacking headlong into a wall? Take a look at the following chart to see the gory details. Except for financial well-being and a few other things, I was *not* a happy camper. When it came to what were supposed to be the *fun* things in my new life—my social connections, being productive and creative, being intellectually stimulated—I felt even worse off than I did during the most demanding periods of my career! It's fair to say, I was anything but grounded. Fortunately, graphing this out spurred me to change, and soon I began to turn the corner.

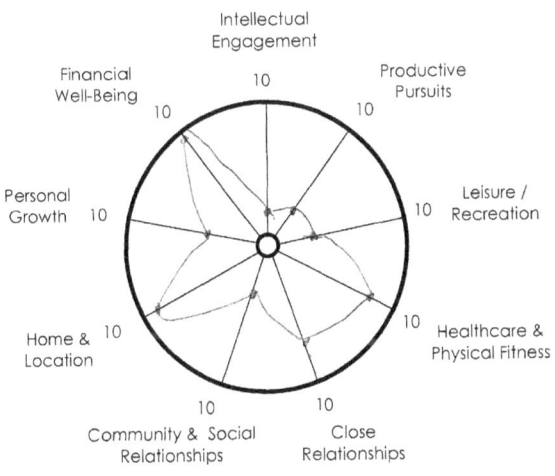

BRINGING MONEY + LIFE INTO FOCUS

Wheel of Retirement

Client Name MICHAEL KAY   Date 5/2.1

Directions: This exercise will help you to assess your growth and development in each Facet of Life in Retirement. It will also help you to evaluate the degree of balance and level of life satisfaction you are now experiencing.

Step #1—Place a dot on each spoke that indicates your level of satisfaction in that particular Facet of Life. Use a scale of 0 to 10 with 0 at the hub and 10 at the rim. A zero indicates no satisfaction and a ten indicates the highest degree of satisfaction.

Step #2—Now draw a line to connect the dots and create your life wheel.

Step #3—Is your life wheel round or does it show flat spots? Is it deflated or is it full? What does this exercise tell you about your life? Is your life balanced? Are there areas of your life that need attention? In what facets would you like to experience more satisfaction?

Another aspect of groundedness is creating your lists of Dos and Don'ts, in other words, your boundaries. For example, I have stringent guidelines about how I use my time and what I am willing and unwilling to do. I shared earlier my rule about "joy"—if it's not joyful, I'm out. I also decided to separate myself from people who are toxic or who drain my spirit. I don't care about the history between us; I care about devoting my time and energy to people who are positive, engaging, and life-affirming. People who carry their black clouds around with them are strongly on my "don't list." That doesn't mean I abandon people when they're in the midst of difficulty. Far from it! I mean people who historically or chronically behave in a way that is energy-sapping.

There are many opportunities to create boundaries that provide you with guidelines for staying grounded. It all goes back to your values. If you value building relationships, then what are the actions associated with accomplishing that? If you value family, how are you factoring that in your life? You get the picture. Another area to consider as you build your new life might include the number of commitments you're willing to make per day, the types of activities you're willing to explore or do. At all costs, eliminate the "shoulds" from your life. If it's a "should," it's probably not good for you.

I suggest you create a list of your dos and don'ts to help you stay grounded in your life. For example, here's a worksheet to help you put your thoughts on paper. Believe me, you'll want to refer back to these worksheets as changes are expected, and a memory refresher can be invaluable.

Creating meaningful boundaries is an important reminder to keep yourself from losing focus on the critical areas. While this part of your life is filled with exploration, you want to know that you are living your values and remaining true to who you are and what you want (and what you don't want) going forward.

EXERCISE #5

Your 3 Dos and Your 3 Don'ts

What are your 3 dos?

_____

_____

_____

_____

_____

_____

_____

_____

What are your 3 don'ts?

_____

_____

_____

_____

_____

_____

_____

_____

The Power of the Growth Mindset

After decades of work, family life, and life's challenges, it's not a stretch to think that you might just want to coast a bit, reduce the turmoil, and relax. Getting stuck in routine or resisting change is perfectly normal. After all, the idea of retirement, at least as framed by society's definition, is a time to step away from life's problems. I've heard from many men I've worked with that the idea of climbing more mountains (in a symbolic sense) just doesn't light them up. But, then, after a time of discussion and exploration, they feel better about having to wrestle the alligator again. I want to assure you, while the idea of change can be challenging, the benefits far outweigh the alternative. You got this!

We arrive in adulthood with a personality. Some of us are more optimistic, while others are less so. Some of us love routine, while others feel dread. Life can build us up or hammer us into submission. But according to the research, *how* we think about life has an immense impact on our happiness and success. While it is true that some evidence suggests cognitive flexibility and openness to change may decline with age, substantial data also challenge this stereotype.

Research shows that the brain retains plasticity well into older age, especially when learning is self-directed and meaningful.[6] An article published in 2025 in *The Gerontologist*, titled "Patterns of Perceived Control That Buffer Against Cognitive Decline in Midlife and Old Age,"[7] found that perceived control, purpose,

---

6 Patrice Voss, Maryse E. Thomas, J. Miguel Cisneros-Franco, and Etienne de Villers-Sidani, "Dynamic Brains and the Changing Rules of Neuroplasticity: Implications for Learning and Recovery," *Frontiers in Psychology,* 2017. Vol. 8, article 1657, doi:10.3389/fpsyg.2017.01657.

7 Jeremy M. Hamm, K. Parker, Margie E. Lachman, J.A. Mogle, K.A. Duggan, and R. McGrath, "Patterns of Perceived Control That Buffer Against Cognitive Decline in Midlife and Old Age," *The Gerontologist,* 2025. Vol. 8, issue 7, doi: 10.10193/geronb/gbafo81.

and relevance were better predictors of openness to change than mere age. When older adults feel a change is aligned with their values, they show strong engagement and flexibility.

Seeing the world and our place in it positively is truly necessary for making this life stage successful.

Maintaining a growth mindset is vitally important as you navigate this transition. Carol Dweck's book *Mindset: The New Psychology of Success* is a great place to start if you haven't read it or need to revisit it. The book covers the idea of how people tend to have either a fixed or a growth mindset. The fixed mindset believes that abilities are static, avoids challenges, is defensive, and fears failure. In contrast, a growth mindset holds that abilities can be developed through effort and perseverance, embraces challenges, is resilient, and enjoys the effort of challenging itself.

A growth mindset is a must-have if you want to successfully lean into this next chapter and has vast implications in every aspect of life. You will need to engage your self-awareness muscle, as discussed in Chapter 3, to determine whether you need a tune-up in this area. Asking yourself reflective questions can be a great tool in staying on course. For example, when presented with change or a looming possibility, notice your initial reaction. If it's negative, ask yourself why and where your response is coming from. Ask: "Am I being close-minded or open-minded?" You might need to sit with it and let the idea marinate before deciding whether to take the leap or not. Remember, you now have the privilege of time for contemplation and examination. Don't underestimate the power of giving an idea time and space for due consideration.

One man I coached expressed his desire to learn pottery because he was interested in pursuing something creative and recalled his experience as a child at camp. When I asked whether he had found a studio, he seemed to turn off. After further inquiry, it turned out that he was afraid to look incompetent in a class (an example of that self-judging, lifelong monster of ego, identity, and self-esteem rearing its ugly head). He resisted putting himself in a situation where he didn't feel competent. Fortunately, after reviewing his values (creativity, bravery), he took the leap. He came away amazed that no one was watching him, being engrossed in their own projects. But it was his bridge to cross, one that he initially decided to avoid.

The art of noticing is a great habit to try to hardwire into your being. It's the cornerstone for developing strong self-awareness. Unfortunately, we don't practice this skill very often when it doesn't pertain to our everyday life. Here are a few examples, from the outside and inside. You wake up in the morning and notice frost on the window. It tells you how to dress for the day. After eating a heavy meal for dinner, you notice that you're not sleeping well and your stomach is upset. These examples are pretty clear. But what about noticing your temperament, noticing your disposition? If you've had a crappy night's sleep because of that very rich meal, and you get up in the morning feeling poorly, do you take those clues and intentionally factor in the necessity to walk into the office and not bite someone's head off for no good reason? You have the ability to take information and adjust your thinking and behavior based on what needs to be done. You might have enjoyed a hugely successful career, but you may notice how woefully inadequate you feel when moving forward positively in retirement. You might notice that you are not displaying a growth mindset. We have the choice of how we view ourselves and our circumstances. But first, we need the self-awareness to even bring such decisions to the table.

Generativity: Leaving Your Mark on the Future

Generativity is the desire to connect to the world positively. It refers to the concern for establishing, nurturing, and guiding the next generation. It's the desire to leave a legacy, contribute to society, and create something that lives beyond you. Have you ever asked yourself questions like: "Why was I put on this earth?", "Did my being here matter?", "Did my life mean anything?"

Time to hit up the worksheet on generativity (see next page). You've got two questions to ponder:

1. Who, or what, can benefit from the generosity of time, knowledge, experience, resources, creativity, love, and passion?
2. In what ways can you use your generosity of time, knowledge, experience, resources, creativity, love, and passion that align with your values?

These are big, meaningful questions. You should address them the same way you'd approach eating an elephant: one bite at a time.

In my life as a financial life planner, the question of financial legacy was a frequent conversation. But it rarely, if ever, breached the walls beyond into the bigger questions. Working through these issues requires introspection and a firm grasp on what you value. Maybe this is a good time to review what you've written about your personal values? Think about how to take those values and align them with your actions.

As I mentioned earlier, a big stumbling block for some is the notion that giving back means making a global impact. If that describes you, well, my friend, maybe it's time to go back and reread the section on groundedness. Let me reframe things for you: think local! The most significant and most assured-of-success impact you can have on the world is with the people in

EXERCISE #6

Generativity: How Can I Help?

Who, or what, can benefit from your generosity of time, knowledge, experience, resources, creativity, love, and passion?

_____

_____

_____

_____

_____

_____

_____

In what ways can you use your generosity of time, knowledge, experience, resources, creativity, love, and passion that align with your values?

_____

_____

_____

_____

_____

_____

_____

your life and your immediate community. Trust me, those efforts, whether you see them or not, will ripple in their own way out into the wider world. If you are in that rarified position to make an impact of a greater proportion, well, then that's just pretty damn cool. Go for it!

Leaving your mark can be super simple. For example, you can help the next generation achieve success by sharing your wisdom and experience. I heard from one man that while he wanted to help others, he had no interest in working at a food bank. It made me smile. There are endless ways of making a difference. Again, a great place to start is to go back to your *values*. I value spending time with my children and grandchildren. When I am engaged with my grandkids, there is nothing more important to me in that moment. It doesn't matter if I'm pushing them on the swings or watching a show with them. I am there, fully and completely. I know several men who volunteer in organizations like SCORE, where they can use their experience to help young entrepreneurs. It doesn't matter what you do, big or small—what matters is that it's something that aligns with your values.

My friend Marty devotes time to installing smoke detectors for the Red Cross. My friend and college roommate, Rick, is putting effort into fixing and restoring an old one-room synagogue in a summer beach community. Another friend, Phil, devotes his energies to raising funds for Diabetes Research. I know another member of the Chapter X community who pitches in at a local food bank. Each one of these actions is personal, meaningful, and important in their lives.

I guess this is as good a time as any to mention the idea of legacy (just a quick note for now; I promise to take a deeper dive into this area later). As you think about your life up to now, you have been building your legacy. You know, as a spouse/partner, a father, a colleague, a boss, a co-worker, a friend . . . but now you get to work on who you are as a human and how you touch those who are meaningful to you. You get to sign the lower right-hand corner of the canvas that is the masterpiece of your life story: the successes, the failures, how you showed up, your learning, your growth, your love . . . . It's a lot to digest. I guess, if you want, you can work to be remembered as a great doctor, executive, lawyer, or someone who worked enormous hours to provide for your family. You get to decide what's important to you. Think about it.

Just as you navigated your work life with purpose, learning, curiosity, and passion, life in Chapter X requires the same level of care, preparation, and love. You have the tools, or at least most of them. Those that need some attention are just part of the growth process. You've done it before. You can do it now.

A VIEW FROM CHAPTER

"Three Keys to Success in Retirement" by Phil Wisoff

As I think of it, for me, there are three ways that make me feel successful at this stage of my life:

1. Physical Well-Being: Am I taking care of myself in ways that make me feel healthy and capable of doing the things that I want? I get a great deal of satisfaction knowing that I am being successful at this particular aspect of living. At this stage of life, we all have physical limitations of some sort. But are we working within those limits to be our best physical selves? And even with these limits, there is always something to strive for.

2. Supporting People: Being there for the people whom I have a strong bond with (be they family or friends). I feel successful knowing that I have been helpful or supportive of these people. When they come to me for support or advice, it gives me satisfaction knowing that they think of me in that way.

3. Creating Bonds and Friendships: At this stage of life, it is sometimes difficult to meet new people and develop relationships (remember how easy it was to do in college and grade school). It is more difficult now, but when I do, it can be very rewarding. Also, it does sometimes force you to try new things (or put yourself out there) in order to meet and connect. I have to admit, on this one, I am not very proactive, trying to meet new people, and I depend more on serendipitous events to make this happen. But when it does happen, I have a feeling of success.

CHAPTER 7

Other Tools in Your Collection

"The mind that opens to a new idea never
returns to its original size."
—*Albert Einstein, physicist*

In the previous two chapters, we've discussed the wide variety of tools you likely possess to help you make the most out of your Chapter X—tools like resilience, problem-solving, flexibility, creativity, groundedness, communication, learning, generativity, and purposeful action. I hope by now you recognize that you have these resources at your disposal. This tool chest is a part of your accumulated wisdom, which you've been gathering since childhood. In this chapter, we will talk about some other tools that are mighty allies in your quest to live life to its fullest.

Engage Life with a Sense of Humor

The first thing that comes to mind is a sense of humor. Wow, I cannot say enough about how important humor is in thriving. Working with the Chapter X community has made it clear that some of us are deadly serious in how we navigate challenges, while others seem to have a more carefree attitude. I will say this as strongly as I can: if you haven't learned to laugh at yourself by now, your road ahead promises to be a lot more difficult than it needs to be.

I promise, you will need a good sense of humor, about yourself and the world in general, if you're going to find the happiness and peace of mind you deserve. Taking yourself too seriously leads to a lack of perspective, reduced resilience, strained relationships, inflexibility, and a diminishment of creativity and joy. And it can make dealing with change all the more difficult. Let's face it, many of the feelings of the perceived harm we experience need to be laughed off as unimportant.

If you struggle with taking yourself too seriously, don't panic. Here are a few ideas to consider.

- Practice gentle, self-deprecating humor. Laugh at your quirks and imperfections.

- Seek honest feedback. Ask people you trust or find a therapist.

- Play more. Try something new, do things that are just for fun. After all, there's *nothing* at stake other than experiencing the joy of engaging. If you don't like it or fail at it, who cares? Chuckle at yourself and move on to the next fun experience.

- Reframe mistakes in a positive way. Look at errors as learning and not an indictment of your failures. Be willing to forgive yourself and grow from the experience.

- Surround yourself with lighthearted people. After all, laughter, they say, is contagious.

- Engage in mindfulness or self-reflection. Think about what the ego is (you know, that sense of self-importance that is glued to us like a second skin) and what your essence or true self is.

- Remind yourself that—get ready—you are *not* the center of the universe. Get over it!
- Celebrate your imperfections. Celebrate your humanness.

As I've shared before, I was a serious trumpet student as a teen. Working with a super-demanding teacher, I was driven to succeed, and nothing other than perfect was acceptable. To top it off, my father was very demanding and made it clear that if my grades didn't reach an *A*, they weren't good enough. I still have the internal scars that I have borne since childhood of never being good enough. While I loved music and playing, I was never satisfied.

When I started playing again a few years ago, I initially went back to the old habits of self-criticism and self-loathing. My friend, the famous musician and music educator Justin DiCioccio, who encouraged my return to playing, kept reminding me to "have fun," "there's nothing at stake," and "find the joy in the music." I wrote down his encouraging messages and taped them to my music stand. Every time I miss a note or screw up a passage, I look at his words to remind me to laugh at my mistakes and smile.

After a lifetime of trying to reach the top or find success in our profession, we get to loosen the reins and laugh, smile, have fun, make mistakes—all under the umbrella of learning, improving, and leaving our self-inflated ego at the office. That "thing" (our ego) that we've guarded and groomed so carefully throughout our teens and career needs to be diminished to allow our true selves to emerge. Do you remember the joy of playing and having fun as a child? That's what you're reaching for here. A return to simple, basic, nonjudgmental, joyful, self-loving fun!

If you've never read David Sedaris' book *Me Talk Pretty One Day*, I suggest you pick it up as a primer for laughing at oneself.

We are all flawed, fallible, and finite! It's part of being human. Let's celebrate it!

Courage Is Still Your Ally

Courage is another tool or attribute that is so vitally important. Think about all the times the only thing that stood between you moving forward and standing still was your courage to take that next step forward. Aging is not easy, even if you're trying to stay fit, healthy, and in command of your faculties. It takes intention and attention. Even with all your efforts, you are ultimately fighting a battle that cannot be won; at least not forever. You can try and hide, you can seal yourself away in a safe room, but changes, challenges, loss, heartache, worry, and illness are all on the horizon to one degree or another. You can face it, like you've faced so many challenges before, with courage or not. It's a choice, right?

Can you think of an example of where you were courageous? I recalled a moment when, as an accountant, I was called to court for the first time on a divorce case to testify on the report I'd prepared. I was told by the attorney who'd hired the firm that the opposing counsel would attack my work, highlight my youth and relative inexperience, and try to trip me up, confuse me, and basically make me look foolish. I remember standing outside the courtroom feeling really scared. The client's financial life depended on the outcome of this case. There was a part of me that was ready to do a quick 180 and run. But I found the courage to open the door and walk into court. And my courage sustained me, helped me hold my ground during testimony, and defend the client's interests.

We all have stories that demonstrate the gut-check time when we wanted to curl up in a fetal position, but instead figured out how to stand tall and do what needed to be done. I remember hearing the expression "gird your loins," which comes from some biblical reference. I never knew that it actually meant to tie your tunic around your hips, but it basically meant to get your ass ready, some shit is coming down. I've spoken to men who have lost their wives to illness, and they had to figure out how to keep going. Several of the men in the Chapter X community have shared their cancer diagnoses or other challenges with which they've been confronted. We all have had them. Think about it: What is the alternative to marshalling your internal strength and—you'll excuse the reference to Chapter 5—using your problem-solving ability, your flexibility, resilience, and so on to deal with the problem at hand? You want to use as many of your tools as possible to meet a challenge. Courage will always be part of that mix.

Patience and Curiosity Help Smooth Things Out

There are other tools, like patience and curiosity, that are invaluable allies in your search for meaning, purpose, and joy. When I look in the mirror, I see someone who is incredibly curious, but also extremely impatient. I'm the guy at the lavish buffet who can't wait to try everything and impatiently waits to be admitted to the line. I'm also the guy who gets full after three bites and then grouses about not being able to fit more on the plate. OK, it's paradoxical, but I think many men can relate to the way I think and act.

Curiosity is one of those attributes that is a call to action. The other day, a friend of mine, in a most off-handed way, mentioned his interest in learning to blow glass. I whipped out ChatGPT and provided him, unasked, two glass-blowing locations within 30 minutes of his home. I can't wait to find out whether he's taken any action. In the words of The Most Interesting Man in the World, "Stay thirsty, my friend."

Do you remember as a child exploring the nearby woods? I do. I remember turning over rotted logs and rocks, curious as to what lay beneath. I remember wondering what would happen if we dammed up the stream that ran through that part of the woods, watching as a pool formed, and spotting tadpoles and other creatures in the water. I watched my granddaughter mix yellow and blue, and the look on her face when green magically arrived. The point is: there is no ceiling to curiosity; there's only the experience of finding out. I guess a minor footnote is essential here: you might be curious about what it is like in outer space, but that's where "groundedness" comes into play; it just might not be possible to explore everything to every degree.

I admit to having a bit of ambivalence when it comes to patience, but I recognize the need to tamp down the exuberance when appropriate. I guess I've always been that guy who sees a situation and focuses on the action that needs to be taken. Patience, though, is one of those attributes that provides space for contemplation, analysis, and consideration, and I see the benefits clearly. One of the Chapter X men I spoke with told me about a situation where his child was seeking guidance. His initial reaction was to give him what was asked; instead, he told his son to sit with the problem for a little while and come back to him with some possible solutions or ideas. It worked like a charm, and everyone benefited greatly. My friend, instead of providing immediate input, allowed his son the opportunity to think, consider, and develop a pathway solely his own. It was a lesson in active patience.

Patience provides spaciousness to allow thoughts and information to marinate, enabling them to come from a place of considered wisdom rather than reaction. I am, like all of us, in one way or another, a work in process in this department. It is closely aligned with self-awareness. Being mindful enough to recognize when to hit the "pause" button before acting or speaking provides countless dividends.

I am sure you can come up with other tools or attributes that resonate with you. But lastly, I want to talk about gratitude as a valuable tool to enlist as you move forward. Gratitude is a transformative mindset. It shifts your focus from loss to possibility and leads directly to the creation of meaning. Gratitude allows you to see yourself as more than what's been lost and to find something positive in any situation. Gratitude is not a denial of hardship, and it's not a phony put-on-a-happy-face mask. It's the realization that you're still standing, and that you have the opportunity to move forward. I think we can agree that holding onto, honing, and recognizing gratitude is a key tool needed in finding and creating joy.

Gratitude

A gratitude practice is a great way to ensure you experience a bit of this profound emotion each day. Some keep a journal and record what they feel grateful for each day. It might be as simple as feeling grateful for your last inhale and exhale, for the sun and the flowers in the garden, for your health and those you love. It could be feeling grateful for something big, like your spouse or children, or an old friend's recovery from a tough illness.

Many research studies document the benefits of gratitude. One example is the Emmons and McCullough study that found that participants who kept gratitude journals reported greater well-being, exercised more, had fewer physical complaints, and were more optimistic.[8] So many benefits came from such a small, daily habit. I'd sign up for that right now!

Another meaningful study, "Gratitude and Well-Being: A Review and Theoretical Integration,"[9] found that gratitude correlates with better mental health, sleep, and relationships.

Finally, mechanisms whereby gratitude may relate to well-being discussed, including schematic biases, coping, positive affect, and broaden-and-build principles.

Establishing a gratitude practice might include journaling, saying daily affirmations, writing letters of gratitude, or focusing mindfully on gratitude during meditation or walks. There are also a plethora of gratitude apps out there, like Gratitude, Presently, or Three Good Things, to help you along.

Clearly, you have tools in your kit that you might not even have realized were there. The big work here is to sit with all this information, consider what *you* need right now, and figure out how to integrate it into something usable. Remember our friendly neighborhood elephant that's sitting there on the plate? One small bite at a time.

---

8 R.A. Emmons & M.E. McCulloch, 2003). "Counting Blessings versus burdens: An experimental investigation of gratitude and subjective well-being in daily life." Journal of Personality and Social Psychology, 84(2), 377-389. httos://doi.org/10.1037/0022-3514.84.2.377.

9 A.M. Wood, J.J. Froh, and Adam Geraghty, 2010. "Gratitude and Well-Being: A Review and Theoretical Integration," *Clinical Psychology Review*, PMID: 20451313 DOI: 10.1016/j.cpr.2010.03.005.

A VIEW FROM CHAPTER

"What I've Learned" by Phillip Bank

In 1969, my aunt and uncle sent me a gift subscription (as a Bar Mitzvah present) to *Esquire* magazine, which turned into a valuable and transformative tool in my journey to adulthood. Over the years, I've looked forward to each new issue, especially the "What I've Learned" column, a popular feature of candid interviews with accomplished actors, writers, athletes, musicians, politicians, and other well-known personalities. I've found their insights ranged from amusing and humorous to inspirational and profound. In that same style, here are a few thoughts and reflections from a man of a certain age.

- There are many things that I know now that I wish I had known then. There are also some things I know now that I wish I didn't.

- I've learned much from watching people do things well. I've probably learned more by watching people screw things up.

- It has been said that what doesn't kill you makes you stronger, though sometimes what doesn't kill you can really piss you off.

- Persistence is a key to success. Sometimes a no is a no. Sometimes it just means "not today."

- In the long run, value is more important than cost.

- It's not important to win every argument or be right all the time. But it's a good idea to be right most of the time.

- Humor (and a smile) can be used to diffuse lots of difficult situations. The ability to make others laugh is a wonderful gift to share: high value, no cost.

- Good health is a gift to be treasured every day, even when you don't feel like it. While not always in our control, do what you can to maintain it.

- My mother says that to have a friend, you have to be a friend. I appreciate all of my friends more than I ever tell them.

- No time? There are 168 hours in a week. If you work 40 hours and sleep 50, that leaves 78 hours a week (118 hours for retirees!). Choose to make good use of it.

- I married the right person. This may be the most important thing I've done and the best advice I can offer others.

CHAPTER 8

Leaning into Change

> **"It is not the strongest or the most intelligent who will survive, but those who can best manage change."**
> —*Charles Darwin, naturalist and geologist*

Everything we've talked about so far in this book can be summed up by one word: *change*. Change is one of those trigger words that is guaranteed to make you squirm, head to the nearest distraction, or run in the opposite direction. It engages that part of our caveman brain that seeks protection. *Hey, you're safe from tigers and other man-eating creatures here in the cave. Don't go outside. It's nice here. There's a fire, and you have some of the berries you found yesterday.* But I am here to tell you, your soul is going to die if you stay put.

I've heard from many men the multitude of reasons, excuses, justifications, and explanations why leaving decades of their work is a bad idea.

"I still like what I do."

"I don't know how I'll fill my day."

"I'm afraid I'll waste away and die when I leave."

They go on and on, but you get the point. I want to get this out and make it clear: if you are still desperately passionate about your work, then I have nothing to say and definitely would not try to dissuade you. The question here is whether you are truly honest with yourself, or if it's just a story you're telling yourself to avoid the discomfort of change. Our caveman brain is really good at telling us why change is a terrible idea. Your job is to discern what is true and what is not.

The other Chapter X non-starter is if your reason to keep working is financial, then, well, you absolutely do need to keep going (which can be good or bad). While this book assumes you have financial security and you've made sure that that aspect of your life is well buttoned down, I implore you to work with a qualified, caring, fee-only financial planner who actually knows how to listen. Nothing is more intrinsic to your well-being than being able to put your head on the pillow at night knowing you're OK financially. Again, it is an alignment of your values with reality. But I will tell you that some people who carry their broken money scripts will never have enough money. Trust me, I've seen this from people who couldn't spend their wealth in three lifetimes, but their sense of fear and dread (that typically came from childhood trauma around money) is still very potent. This is where a qualified therapist can be beneficial, along with a planner who knows their business.

I can tell you from vast experience, some won't get a last will and testament drafted because there's a piece of their belief structure that equates the act with imminent death. The same holds for those who cannot come to terms with seeing life after career as anything other than a death sentence. I hold firmly to the belief that you can have and deserve to have a post-career life filled with meaning, purpose, and joy—if you're willing to do the work. If you're willing to change again.

Friedrich Nietzsche said, "No price is too high to pay for the privilege of owning yourself." Yup, Freddie was a pretty smart dude. "Owning yourself" falls very neatly into the idea of self-actualization, which is associated with the work of Abraham Maslow. *Self-actualization* refers to the full realization and expression of one's talents, capabilities, and potential. Now ask yourself: Does your work-life bring you to the apex of your potential?

If you hold to the idea that we are always returning—you know, the ashes-to-ashes idea that we return to where we began—then it seems to me that there's an appropriate place and space between work and death. A return, as it were, to exploration, fun, joy, purpose, delight, curiosity, innocence, creativity, and lack of financial responsibility—a place we haven't known since childhood. I can't think of anything sadder than someone who works until they become infirm and have therefore lost their chance to reclaim themselves.

What stands between this "return" to oneself and you? It's probably that caveman that still resides inside that part of your brain, keeping you inside, eating old berries. The amygdala is the part of the brain responsible for the fight, flight, or freeze responses, and while it might be helpful in a dark alley or in the jungle, it's friggin' useless to you in this situation. While it has all good intentions, it nudges you just enough to pull back. That cloying fear that keeps you in place has, I'll guess, made its presence felt in your past.

The feeling of discomfort tells you to stay put or run like hell. But I am here to tell you that it's time to fight. The battle of You vs. Your Amygdala is *on*! If you're not careful, your amygdala is going to "layeth the Smackdown on your candy ass." (OK, another pop culture reference . . . sometimes, I can't resist). Way back in 1991, Albert Brooks wrote and starred in a fantastic movie, *Defending Your Life*. If you've never seen it, I can't encourage you enough to watch it. The point was that when you die, your soul goes to a place to be judged on whether you've been able to overcome fear in your past life, in order to move forward. Overcoming fear is big work; it's never an easy task. But if you're honest, I bet you can write a book on all the times you've done it in the past.

Think about it. In fact, let's go one better; grab your pencil and paper, and think about some of the highlights of your ability to conquer your fears. Come on, you know, first time being called to the blackboard in school to solve a problem; first time you called a girl on the phone to ask for a date, first day of college, first day of work, keep going. All that discomfort that felt like an unscalable wall, but that you still leaped over. What pushed you over the top?

I'm not playing the role of judge here. But I would like you to dig into the following exercise.

- What makes you uncomfortable: I want you to imagine something that makes you squirm with discomfort. What is it? What feelings does it bring up for you? Try to really lean into the experience of imagining this activity or action. Describe it in vivid detail. Where in your body do you feel it? What do you do with it?

- What are the consequences of trying something that makes you uncomfortable? What do you have to lose? What might you gain? Think about a time when you pushed out of your comfort zone. Was it near-fatal? What did you learn about yourself?

- What are the consequences of *not* trying something that makes you uncomfortable? Surely, you've had experiences when you made the decision not to try something. Did you experience any regrets? It might be easy to blow it off by telling yourself you just didn't want to try that some-thing, but I'll bet there have been instances where you had

EXERCISE #7

Facing Discomfort

What makes you uncomfortable?

_____

_____

_____

_____

_____

What are the consequences of trying something that makes you uncomfortable?

_____

_____

_____

_____

_____

_____

What are the consequences of NOT trying something that makes you uncomfortable?

_____

_____

_____

_____

_____

_____

second thoughts. Write about that in as much detail as possible.

What did you learn from this exercise? What are the takeaways? How can you take what you've learned and use it to bolster your courage, resolve, and willingness to venture out of your comfort zone?

For some, the idea of walking into a roomful of strangers is intolerable. For others, being terrible at something makes them cringe. Maybe, for you, the idea of picking up the phone and connecting with an old friend or walking up to a stranger at a coffee shop and starting a conversation makes you think of the benefits of bingeing Netflix. The reality is you have nothing at stake. You won't lose the love of your grandkids, your portfolio will not drain, and you won't be airlifted for emergency surgery. Most often, there's literally nothing at stake to do something outside of your comfort zone, especially because you've done *so many* things in your life that took you outside of your comfort zone. It takes self-awareness and courage, first to recognize your discomfort, and then even more to push yourself beyond your comfort zone. But, really, you only have one life. What are you waiting for? I challenge you to go to a nursing home or assisted living facility and ask the residents about their regrets. It's too late for them (by and large), but not for you!

What is needed is the ability to look within yourself and honestly explore what's going on. What are the blocks? What's real versus what's just an unfounded fear or resistance point? You have the keys to the 1964 Aston Martin DB5 (or the DeLorean, if you must); you can take it out for a spin or leave it in the garage. Your choice!

Change Brings Wonderful Possibilities

As you prepare to embark on your next chapter, devote as much time as possible to contemplating your truths, such as your fears, self-imposed limitations, and expectations for your life in the future. As you build this out, there's another component that needs to be addressed: your list of possibilities.

I love my list of possibilities; I've had one for years. It's my list of things I'd like to explore. My list consists of places I'd like to see and why. It also contains stuff like learning another language, making chocolate, getting a master's in fine arts, taking my family to Israel, spending a month in Italy, going back to India to attend yoga and meditation classes, doing the Bourbon Trail and the Baseball Hall of Fame with my son (not on the same trip), learn how to make pottery, be invited to do a TedTalk. My list goes on and on.

The great thing about having a list of possibilities is that you can add or delete anything at any time. There's no penalty for not doing something that at one time seemed like a good idea. At one time, I had considered competing in my age group in weightlifting, but my cardiologist put an end to that. Oh, well, life goes on, and I'm still standing. As Dirty Harry said, "A man's got to know his limitations." Many people do not have a list of possibilities simply because they have had no time while they're working to even think about it. So their natural default is to say, "Play golf" or "I'll keep working."

If you don't have a list, it's time to start (turn the page for the worksheet). All you need is something to write with, something to write on, and a distraction-free space. Believe it or not, I do my best thinking and writing with music on (yes, Foo Fighters). For some reason, silence is more distracting to me. But you need to find the right atmosphere that promotes your ability to think, imagine, ponder, and write. Here are some prompts:

- ✖ What might be fun?
- ✖ What might be interesting?
- ✖ What aligns with my values?

Once you finish, go back and see if you can tie in a "why" to each entry. I like Simon Sinek's work around your "why." I don't particularly subscribe to the idea that you *need* to start there, but at some point in the process, you'll need to answer that question. You want to connect your life decisions and actions back to your values. If you can't connect the dots, then one of two possibilities exists. First, maybe you haven't identified why you value something. You might need to add another item to your values list. Second, it's not something you care that much about, and while it's fine to explore something new, you will want to make sure there's alignment. Remember my example about playing with the community band? I love playing my instrument, but the music and the people were not joy-fuel for me. My action was to say no!

Getting Out of Your Comfort Zone

Here's a hard fact: no one ever died from being uncomfortable. But if your amygdala chases you into a corner to hide, then you get to miss out on all the fun, learning, creativity, joy, and possibilities that are derived from new experiences. Exercise #9 (turn the page) will help you explore this. As you think about what creates discomfort in you, I'd like you to match up your list of possibilities and consider your level of discomfort in embarking on this adventure. For example, if you list something like running a marathon or hiking the Appalachian Trail, think about what you need to accomplish it and where any discomfort lies. Locate the resistance and dig deeper into how you might achieve this possibility so that the challenge is more of a mole hill than a

EXERCISE #8
Your Possibilities List

A space to imagine activities or endeavors that could bring you joy, spark curiosity, or feel meaningful. Use this page to begin your exploration.

What might be fun?

_____

_____

_____

_____

_____

What might be interesting?

_____

_____

_____

_____

What aligns with my values?

_____

_____

_____

_____

_____

mountain. Remember where I talked about the microscopic aperture of your lens as you sit in mastery. In your Chapter X, you need to widen that lens to see more of yourself, your limiting beliefs, and your inner fears that keep you locked in place.

Breaking through resistance (discomfort) can be accomplished by first identifying what the resistance is and why. Is it fear? Uncertainty? Perfectionism? The next steps include breaking down the challenges into small, manageable parts and practicing self-compassion—so you don't beat yourself up! Use words that are affirming and that don't feed into defeatist thinking. For example, instead of "I'm anxious," use "I'm excited to try something new" or "I am interested in discovering how I can stretch myself in positive ways."

To live your next chapter fully, you will need to challenge your comfort zone time and time again. Remember we talked about having a growth mindset? Well, that's what is needed to push through the barrier of discomfort. It takes a higher level of self-awareness to identify these feelings and put them in the correct context. As I mentioned earlier in the book, I have found that journaling helps me reflect on these ideas. Journaling is great because it allows you to ponder, think, and consider what's really going on inside. I know you're a tough guy, but it's OK to be fearful, weak, unsure, and human, at least on paper—just to yourself. Admittedly, I am also a big fan of working with a therapist when the knots are just too tight and you need some help in untangling them. If you are married or partnered, engaging in rich, meaningful conversations can be so helpful. If you are not, having good friends with whom you are close enough to spill is a gift beyond measure when it comes to getting out of your head.

One of the men in the X community found that he soon panicked after retiring because he had set unreasonable expectations and was confronted by more change than he could

EXERCISE #9

Getting Out of Your Comfort Zone

What are you willing to commit to that is outside of your comfort zone?

_____

_____

_____

_____

_____

_____

_____

_____

_____

_____

_____

_____

_____

_____

_____

_____

_____

_____

handle. His reaction was to go back to the familiar routine of work; it was simpler and required no risk. It wasn't a money thing; it wasn't even a lack of ideas for activities and projects to keep him engaged. So, what was it? After a few coaching sessions, he realized he had let his fear consume him, which made him very anxious. I suggested he engage with a therapist to help him get untangled. Six months later, he was re-retired and making great strides in creating a life that is uniquely his, one filled with joy. It's not a plug-and-play type of thing—it takes work, self-awareness, courage, and a recognition that discomfort is not the signal for staying in the cave.

You've done an enormous amount of work in Part 2 of this book. You might even be qualified as an archaeologist of sorts, excavating memories, evaluating experiences, cataloging, and categorizing information. Remember, the point is: you have within you most, if not all, of the tools necessary to create a life filled with meaning, purpose, and joy (as you define each).

Did you ever see the movie *Breaking Away*? It was released in 1979 and centered on a group of boys from working-class families in Bloomington, Indiana, who are struggling to find their identity and place in the world—the main character, Dave, played by Dennis Christopher, dreams of becoming a professional cyclist. Without going down the rabbit hole, it was, in my estimation, a terrific movie that dealt with real issues of growing up.

If you tilt the lens ever so slightly, can you see the similarity between the crisis of young adulthood depicted in the film and the process of growing into your next iteration? In both there are so many possibilities, so many emotions, and a good chunk of uncertainty about what the future holds. You've devoted your entire professional life to doing what you do. So how do you "break away" from what you have been to what you need to be going forward?

You've put real effort into answering questions like these in the worksheets dealing with identity, values, and regrets. You've seen how you've used the tools you've developed over your lifetime, like problem-solving, learning, flexibility, resilience, creativity, communications, and understanding purposeful action. You've been introduced to the concepts of groundedness, growth mindset, and generativity—all necessary strengths in developing this new version of you. Additionally, you dug into a few other areas that will help keep you focused on what's really important to you, such as having a good sense of humor (and not taking yourself so seriously), courage to face whatever comes next, and developing curiosity and patience as you explore possibilities, opportunities, and challenges. Finally, we talked about the idea and importance of a simple gratitude practice to be your North Star.

I trust that you worked through these exercises with thoughtful patience (and you can always redo them if you want). Rushing through only detracts from the purpose of laying a new foundation for life after your career. I want you to lean in, as much as possible, to contemplation, self-awareness, mindfulness, and truth-telling. In other words, don't hide behind excuses; don't self-justify. Own your strengths and your weaknesses with honesty, courage, and self-love.

Next Steps

We're at the end of Part 2, and I want to congratulate you for having done such a fantastic job of digging into your past. Part 2 was a deep dive into your memories and all the tools you've perfected throughout your life. In addition to the knowledge, abilities, skills, and habits you've accumulated since childhood, you examined a few more tools, like groundedness, generativity, and the importance of a growth mindset. It's a lot to unpack and assimilate into the new iteration of who you are, a person now without a job/title/familiar identity.

But I'm going to turn the tables on you in Part 3 and have you do a fair bit of future thinking. Fair warning: the next part of the book will start like a cold plunge as you lean into the massive topic of legacy and values. But the work you'll be doing will help point you, with great clarity, toward how you want to live the rest of your life. Then we'll talk about the benefits of establishing balance and boundaries, and finally, we will discuss some of the challenges that lurk in the future that you'll want to be cognizant of. After all, knowing what might arise provides the opportunity for preparation. All the work from Part 2 is preparation for what's next. Are you excited?

But before you turn the page, I ask that you devote a little time (or a lot of time) to appreciating and celebrating your progress. I have been accused of being a terrible self-celebrator. One of the trainings I did during my transition into Chapter X was with BJ Fogg's Tiny Habits Academy. BJ Fogg is a social scientist and researcher at the Stanford Behavior Design Lab. One of the most essential features of successfully acquiring a new habit is to continually celebrate each success, even if it's for one push-up or a single flossed tooth. I want you to do the same; appreciate your efforts. Don't shrug them off as if they are nothing because they *aren't* nothing. The work you put in is something—something big, meaningful, and yours! OK? Get to it!

A VIEW FROM CHAPTER

"Hierarchy of Needs" by Michael Zeldin, PhD

I have worked out a conceptual map of how to use my time and energy in retirement, modeled after Maslow's hierarchy of needs. At the base is health. My first and constant focus is on responding to health challenges so I can have a long "health span" (healthy years ahead of me). This includes taking medications for several chronic conditions and doing what I had to do (surgery and radiation) when I faced prostate cancer a few years ago.

The second tier is wellness. For me, this includes doing things that will better my physical and emotional condition. I exercise several times a week, mostly doing light cardio, but at the urging of one of my physicians, I now include strength training once or twice a week. I maintain the vegetarian diet (more accurately, pescatarian) that I have followed since I was 21. I am quite introspective about my emotional well-being and frequently reach out to friends, my partner, and my therapist for support.

The third tier is relationships. I work hard to express my love for my partner, both as an emotion and in my actions. I stay as close as I can to my family. My daughter, son-in-law, and three of my grandsons live across the street. While we have mutually agreed upon boundaries (e.g., never show up at each other's house without texting first), we see each other often. My second son lives at the other end of the state, and we see him and his family as often as we can, given the busy schedule of a couple with two full-time, high-powered careers and two active children. My third son lives with my partner and me because he has a chronic medical condition. I spend time with him every day, sometimes just a few minutes, but often much longer. He doesn't need help with daily tasks, but he does need help with out-of-the-house errands. More importantly, I try to provide him with loving emotional support as he faces his difficult challenges. Beyond family, we have groups of friends, including a once-a-month group that has gathered for 15 years on Friday nights to celebrate the Jewish Sabbath. And we constantly seek out new friends, some of whom are older than we are and some of whom are younger.

The fourth tier is purpose, which I see as closely related to identity. During my full-time working years, I had a clear sense of purpose. My purpose was to raise the next generation through my teaching, nurturing children who would be filled with joy and a commitment to doing good in the world. I find it more challenging to articulate my purpose now that these two life-animating purposes are somewhat in the background. While I would love to change the entire world for the better, I have developed the wisdom to know that that is beyond my ability. So, my purpose now lies more in spreading kindness and joy among those whose lives I touch. When I pick up my grandchildren from school, I stop asking the meaningless question, "How was school today?" because I know I'll get a meaningless "Fine" as the answer. Instead, I ask, "What did you do today that was kind, or what did you see someone else do that was kind?" This fourth tier is also related to legacy. Part of what I want my grandchildren to take away from their having had me in their lives is the importance of making a difference in people's lives through kindness.

Here, I want to make clear that I don't have in mind a saccharine kindness, but a deeper kindness captured in the spiritual phrase "loving-kindness." One aspect of kindness is clarity (as Brené Brown says, "Clear is kind"), and another is gently challenging people to grow in their knowledge and goodness.

The one essential element of my retirement journey that I can't fit into the hierarchy because it is ever-present in my life is learning. For me, if there's a day when I haven't learned something, it hasn't been a good day. I can learn about retirement, the world, the people in my life, or myself. I can learn from reading, listening to podcasts, or having a conversation with my partner, a friend, or someone I've just met. Learning and growing are what keep each day of retirement fresh and invigorating. Since the journey of learning and growing is never-ending, I imagine that my retirement journey will always remain incomplete.

PART 3
DEFINING YOUR LEGACY

CHAPTER 9

How Do You Want to Be Remembered?

> "Your legacy is being written by yourself.
> Make the right choices."
> —*Gary Vaynerchuk, American businessman
> and author*

Up to this point, you've trusted me to take you on a journey into areas of your memory and aspects of your life that you probably haven't thought about before. I've asked you to recall experiences and draw a solid line between your past and present. I've tossed you down the well of memories, beginning with childhood, and asked you to understand how they connect with who you are today. I've asked you to name your values and even explore your regrets. It's big work.

I can't help thinking about Charles Dickens's *A Christmas Carol*, in which our friend Ebeneezer is allowed to visit his past, see his present, and his inevitable end. The clear lesson: you can take what you've learned, create a vision for a better future, and put the vision into action. Hmmmm . . . it sounds pretty familiar.

Part 2 was crammed with exercises and opportunities to connect the dots to experiences from your life. After all, in all the busyness of living, past experiences tend to fade into an unrecognizable jumble of stuff that "just happened," without consideration of why and how they contributed to the person standing in front of the mirror each morning. With examination, we can make sense of all the twists and turns and uncover who we are once our title, job, occupation, and profession have been eliminated. In addition, we examined the tools we already have and added a few more that will be meaningful from now on. You've harnessed long-forgotten memories that demonstrated your growing competencies in navigating challenges, not to mention the many times you've gone from novice to mastery. You also had the opportunity to think about your values, your dreams, your purpose, and your boundaries. While we can't go back in time and fix our mistakes, misjudgments, and failures, we do, like Ebeneezer, have the opportunity to learn from our past (the good, the bad, and the human) about how best to focus our energy into making the next chapter meaningful.

If you've devoted the appropriate time and focus to the exercises and visualizations in Part 2, you will be ready to jump into this next section. In Part 3, we will talk about your legacy, building a life that works, some potential challenges, self-care, and resilience. Just a reminder: keep your exercises handy in case you need to refresh your memory, re-ground yourself, or stay on course. And don't forget, it's fine to amend your responses when appropriate. Life is fluid, and we need to be adaptable.

My final housekeeping note before we leap into the rest of this chapter is to try to be the "observer" as you proceed. In other words, be mindful of where your emotions and thoughts are coming from (there's that nagging self-awareness thing again). If they are just a reflection of fear (which is simply your caveman brain keeping you away from man-eating dinosaurs and splinters), you can observe the thought, label it as a product of fear, and send it packing. Try also to observe how your body feels as you read through the material. Our bodies and emotions are connected, so you may learn something by paying close attention to the specific physical sensations you experience with certain emotions.

Ready? Of course you are!

Living Your Legacy

During my career, I'd had hundreds of conversations with clients about legacy. But I will freely admit that those conversations were 99% focused on financial legacy; hours of discussion on who would benefit from their success and how it would be distributed. These are serious matters that should not be ignored. But looking back, I find myself wishing we had broadened the scope of what we meant by *legacy*.

The fact is, we leave a legacy that goes far beyond the money, something that touches many different aspects of our lives. I am referring to our personal, professional, and cultural or societal legacy. A cultural or societal legacy refers to enduring acts like founding an institution, advancing social justice, or creating works of art, literature, or science. Our professional legacy defines how we contributed to our field, organization, or cause. It includes the innovations, mentorships, leadership styles, or other contributions we provided that will shape future generations.

The one that perks up a lot of ears, because it's both poignant and motivating, is the focus of this chapter: our personal legacy. In other words, who we are, our values and character, and our beliefs that get passed on to future generations. These are the things that will define how you are remembered by those who matter. I remember my grandfather. He was a tiny man with overly large ears. He spoke with a thick accent and was never without an awful pun and a smile. He loved opera. While my parents definitely lit up my love of music, it was my grandfather who introduced me to opera. I think of him whenever I listen to WQXR on Saturday Opera Afternoon. Bad jokes and opera and a kind smile—I could think of worse legacies.

You might have thought that you were finished with all the heavy lifting of those exercises in the last chapter. Sorry! Grab your writing instrument of choice and paper and . . . ready?. . .

Write your eulogy! No, I'm not joking. I'm going to have you write your own eulogy. Trust me, this is one powerful exercise—I know from personal experience. But to my mind, there's no better way to clarify your legacy.

But don't worry, we're not going to dive straight into that daunting exercise. We'll get there step by step. Before the eulogy, we'll go through two exercises to help firm up your thinking on the subject. The first exercise asks you to answer the question, "Who Am I?" That's followed by an exercise called "What Do I Value?" We'll get through those two first before tackling your eulogy.

Who Am I?

In this exercise, I want you to locate the essence of you, deep in your core, and write a description of who you are or who you aspire to be. What can be more important than to know who you are? If you remember your ancient Greek history, there is a famous quote inscribed at the Temple of Apollo at Delphi: "Know thyself." Isn't that one of the big questions we all want to unravel before we leave? I am going to push the envelope here by reminding you of the quote from Plato's Apology (38a): "The unexamined life is not worth living for a human being."

Allow your mind to focus on the essence of you, your values and the attributes that make you who you are. When I answer this question, I immediately center on the idea of someone who

EXERCISE #10

Who Am I?

Who am I?

_____

_____

_____

_____

_____

_____

_____

_____

_____

_____

_____

_____

_____

_____

_____

_____

_____

_____

_____

wants to help others; someone who is committed to being kind and a supportive ally. What comes to mind when you think about yourself?

This is deep stuff, I know. You'll need to bring all your powers of introspection and discernment to bear. It's not easy work, but give it your best shot.

What Do I Value?

The preceding exercise provided the opportunity to state who you are. The "What Do I Value?" exercise is your opportunity to solidify what you stand for, to define the bedrock of your foundation as a human. After all, your values are what guide your decisions and your actions. If you refer back to your first exercise on values, see if there are any changes to be made or if you were spot on. Consider how the words you put into the mouths of your closest family and friends align with those values. Take as much time as you need to write, in as much detail as necessary, the answer to the question: What do you value?

✖ ✖ ✖

Now that you have created the statements of your identity and the values that surround your being, it's time to get to the big stuff! Writing one's own eulogy is a big ask, especially knowing that, by now, you've embraced the journey we're on together and you want to see this through to a meaningful conclusion. The work I am asking you to do now will require a good amount of time because you'll need to imagine the selected individuals who will deliver your eulogy and the stories they will share about you after your demise. In other words, you need to get into their heads to produce examples that highlight just how important you were in their lives. If you need to take a break before embarking on

EXERCISE #11

What Do I Value?

What do I value?

_____

_____

_____

_____

_____

_____

_____

_____

_____

_____

_____

_____

_____

_____

_____

_____

_____

_____

_____

this, please do so. You need to be as strong, rested, focused, and committed as possible.

⚔ ⚔ ⚔

Imagine you are a disembodied spirit, hanging around for your funeral before you make your last journey to the great beyond. You're sitting (or floating) in the back of the room waiting to hear what those who remain behind are going to say about you. To get the most out of this exercise, I suggest you write several eulogies, one for each person you would want to hear talk about you. For example, spouse, child, grandchild, work colleague, friend—each will get a shot at remembering you. And each will have a slightly different point of view.

What would you like them to say about you? I imagine you'd like to write down the things you'd like hear from them if you were sitting in the room listening; things that are good and pleasing. But you need to go deeper. The eulogy needs to be full of examples of the *values* you embody and how you wish to be remembered. Please take the time to treat this with all the seriousness it demands. After all, what could be more important than creating a blueprint for how you will live your life going forward?

If this is confusing, let me offer a few thoughts. If you value, say, relationships, make sure your eulogy includes examples of who you cherished and how you showed them your love. If you value creativity, describe how and in what ways you've been creative in your life. If you want to make a difference in the world, show examples of things you do or have done to make the world a better place. (Don't get stuck on the word *world*; it doesn't matter how big or small it is.)

Make this document your vision statement, your blueprint, your action list of whom you care about and what you want to do to demonstrate a life fulfilled. Make it hopeful, make it vibrate

EXERCISE #12

Write Your Eulogy

Imagine this person is giving a eulogy at your funeral. What would you most love for them to say about you, your relationship, and the impact you had on their life?

Your spouse/partner

_____

_____

_____

_____

_____

_____

_____

_____

_____

Your children

_____

_____

_____

_____

_____

_____

_____

_____

_____

EXERCISE #12 (continued)

Your grandchildren

_____

_____

_____

_____

_____

_____

Your best friend

_____

_____

_____

_____

_____

Another person who is important to you

_____

_____

_____

_____

_____

_____

with the essence of who you are and who you are becoming in your Chapter X. Allow me to let you in on a secret hope: I hope your eulogy includes words like laughter, fun, joyful, loving, and kind, and is filled with great stories and examples of the difference you'd made to the speaker.

Maybe you're a bit unsure as to why you're going through these challenging exercises, especially the eulogy. If that's the case, the reason is simple: to create the path forward into your next chapter, you want to be crystal clear about the characteristics and values you embody in your actions. In other words, if you value kindness, I am sure those who eulogize you will be talking about and giving examples of your kindness. You see, your values are expressed in your actions. In your work life, if you valued success, I am sure you can describe in great detail how you achieved it, along with all the hard work and sacrifices that brought you that success. All this work culminates in helping you define "who you are," a question you undoubtedly have ping-ponged in your brain at various times in your life.

A Blueprint for Life

OK, you've done amazing work here, and you probably deserve a break. It's perfectly alright if a tear or two emerged as you leaned into this exercise. This is not exactly like watching *The Simpsons*; it's monumental, big stuff. In fact, as I've mentioned, it is a vital blueprint for the rest of your life. And that—in case you're wondering—is the entire point of this exercise.

You might be dealing with the sobering thought that the current *you* doesn't quite match up to the you described in your glowing eulogy. Don't worry. This is an excellent example of a maxim from Stephen Covey's *The Seven Habits of Highly Effective People*: "Begin with the END in mind." Once you've caught your breath and reapplied your makeup (that was a joke), I'd like you to go back to the document and circle the words that stand out. Words like *loving, caring, creative, helpful, smart, inventive, comforting*, etc., and make note of these words.

Use these words to begin to craft the actions that demonstrate them, either directly or indirectly, to others. For example, if you wish to be remembered as someone loving and caring, jot down ways that you can show it. Spending time with those you love is certainly a top-of-the-list action. How does that fit into the life you're building? If it's creative, what are some of the meaningful ways you can live that?

Remember, time is a factor here. We don't know how long we will be healthy and able. We don't know when our last breath will be taken. Building a life of meaning and purpose can't wait for *some time* in the future when you get around to it. I was talking to my college roommate, whom I consider to be my best friend. He recently retired after a very successful career in accounting and finance. He embodies the idea of "leaving it all on the field." He worked like a madman from his first day at Ernst and Whinney to his retirement from an international nonprofit. He knew, with great clarity, that he now wanted to devote the bulk of his time to his wife, children, and grandchildren. But he needed to start by organizing and sorting things that had accumulated unreviewed for decades. You know, the boxes of memories stashed in the basement or attic. In fact, he sent me a picture of his old clock radio that sat on his college desk and offered a blaring wake-up alarm each morning. I can hear the sound in my head and feel the same dread! Another major project was to ensure his financial and estate information was organized and cataloged for the benefit of whoever survives him. He clearly values making life easier for those he leaves behind.

Another friend of mine is committed to remembering our country's veterans. During the holiday season, he visits cemeteries to place wreaths on the graves. It is deeply meaningful, and his annual pilgrimage to selected cemeteries clearly demonstrates his commitment.

With your blueprint in hand, you have all you need to begin to craft the life you value most . . . the life others will remember you by. But remember, the actions you choose to focus on need to be put in context with all the necessary considerations. I mentioned the word *boundaries* earlier, and I think it's important to dig a little deeper here. It's important to establish your boundaries clearly in this stage of developing your life plan. For example, while you are committed to building, burnishing, or refining your legacy, you need to account for what you'll say no to. For example, do you have the time and resources? Are you physically able? Do you have any messes to clean up first? Are you grounded in the reality of your situation? Once you've gone through all those questions, go for it with passion, meaning, and joy. And don't forget your sense of humor. Are you getting excited, motivated, and focused? Great! Your continued energy and commitment are critical. If you're not, it's time to really think about what's pushing back and why.

In the next chapter, the ideas around finding balance within the confines of appropriate boundaries will be front and center. Oh, don't forget to celebrate! Writing your own eulogy puts you squarely in earthquake territory!

"Life at 75" by Arthur Mack

Retirement for me was something I did look forward to relatively early in my career—say, when I was in my 40s. At that age, my role as a leader in a start-up company required very long hours and lots of travel. Thanks to the support of a great, hard-working team and a strong dose of luck, our efforts were successful enough to command a significant buy-out price from a major company in our industry. What appeared to be good news—and it *was*—was that my equity in the start-up provided a truly life-changing amount of money. Suddenly, the worries of financial security for my family were gone.

Good news, of course. But there was an unexpected downside. As often happens, the buyer of our company had its own leadership team, leaving no room for an outsider at my level. Suddenly, the work I had done—the long hours, the travel, and the leadership position—was gone. I was not who I was anymore in my mid-40s. I had no idea how devastating this would be. Slowing down or retiring provided so much less appeal than it had just a few years before. Who knew? At that point, no amount of money could replace the feeling of "no longer being who I was."

My career resumed with a great deal of hard work and luck. I was able to replace the position I held for 10 years with new opportunities in key leadership roles at start-up companies. And suddenly, I was 70 years of age, and it truly was time to make the transition from the demanding hours and travel. Fortunately, the finances were not an issue, and my health would allow me to pursue an active lifestyle and do some amazing things after my career was over.

But as I experienced in my mid-40s, once again, I was *not* who I was anymore. I had to live with this from now on. I had to allow the younger generations—specifically my kids and kids of friends—to carry on with leadership roles and bright futures, doing what I used to do. Being who I used to be! And I had to learn to keep quiet about who I used to be and how I was who I was. Nobody wants to hear it. I decided that my "glory days" were my days and that my experiences and successes were of very little interest to anyone but me. And finally, five years after retiring, I am living with this as well.

Life in retirement is pretty great after all. We travel whenever and wherever we want to go. We have nine amazing grandchildren, and we actually like them all. We watch as our children thrive in their chosen careers, and now and again, I say to myself, "Ah, they learned so much from watching me in my career on my way up. No wonder they are doing so well!" (I do keep this to myself, though!)

I work part-time in a job that allows me to use some of the skills and knowledge that I gained during my business career and as a former Air Force medic. It's far from a leadership and executive role, as I pack my lunch to eat in the break room during my shifts. My lunches are no longer in a fine restaurant or the executive dining room. That is fine too!

Life at 75 in retirement is wonderful.

CHAPTER 10

. . . .

The Art of Balance: You're in Control of What You're in Control Of

> "Some things are in our control and others not. Things in our control are opinion, pursuit, desire, aversion, and, in a word, whatever are our own actions."
> —*Epictetus, Stoic philosopher*

Countless articles and podcasts have devoted their focus to the idea of "work/life balance." It sounded soooooooooo good! Imagine a life that has the flexibility to serve your needs at the moment. "Sure, I can put off the Board of Directors' meeting to go to my son's T-ball game. No problem!" "Please tell Mrs. Jones that I'll get to her burst appendix when I get back from golf." "Oh, there's a problem with getting our goods through customs, and our biggest customer really needs the order. Tell them I'll get right on it after I get back from vacation."

Well, the real world doesn't exactly work in concert with the idea of work-life balance. But the good news is, in Chapter X, you can actually create a life that suits your wants and desires . . . to a point. It's always "to a point," right? Life after the demands of your profession/occupation changes drastically, and for the most part it's wonderful. There's a freedom that you've never had before, not even in childhood, that awaits you. Getting excited?

Let's start with setting expectations. You might be super pumped to begin your new life without the routine that you've had for the last 40 or 50 years, but no one goes from Alpha to Omega in one breath. Images of ticking things off your bucket list might be dancing in your head, but it takes time to build a new life structure. Right now, you need to think like an architect with a pencil and eraser; you need a concept, a vision, and plans that tell the appropriate story. I talked in an earlier chapter about the idea of boundaries; knowing what you're unwilling to do and what you're not. This is an important distinction from knowing what you are *willing* to do, which, in my thinking, can change like the weather.

I have a few boundaries and one hard and fast rule. I will try anything that seems interesting or fun, but if it's not joyful, I won't do it. *Period!* I love my children and grandchildren and am only too happy to help when needed. But I didn't work my entire life to be a full-time caregiver to my grandchildren. Now, if there's an emergency, I am there, no questions. But my life is mine and I decide how I want to devote the time I have left (with my wife's permission, of course). That's a joke . . . mostly.

Since this whole retirement gig is brand new, it's going to take some time to craft a schedule or routine that works for you. As you lay out your thoughts on paper, add in categories that are important in your life. Use the "Wheel of Life in Retirement" that you worked on earlier as a guide. Pay close attention to areas like health and fitness, relationships, learning, community, financial health, etc. How do these categories fit into your calendar?

EXERCISE #13

Crafting Your Routine

	Mandatory	Very Important	Important	So-So	Not Urgent	Don't Care
Intellectual Engagement						
Productive Pursuits						
Healthcare & Physical Fitness						
Personal Growth						
Financial Well-Being						
Close Relationships						
Home & Location						
Leisure/Recreation						

	Action Steps
Intellectual Engagement	
Productive Pursuits	
Healthcare & Physical Fitness	
Personal Growth	
Financial Well-Being	
Close Relationships	
Home & Location	
Leisure/Recreation	

I have created a very flexible calendar that includes self-care (I work out with a trainer four times a week, get red-light therapy and sauna treatments three times a week). I devote very little time to finances because I have a simple structure that works for me. Everything is on autopay, and I probably devote no more than 30 minutes a week in review. I practice trumpet three to four times a week and attend a weekly rehearsal. I try to have lunch or breakfast with a friend once a week. The rest of my week is devoted to podcasts, writing blogs, time with my family, reading, and pulling weeds in the garden. Even with all this, I still have plenty of time to take a walk, talk with friends, or engage in some of my other hobbies. Now, don't get me wrong—it took some time and effort to get all this figured out. You'll be in the same boat at the beginning, but with some trial-and-error experimentation, you'll figure it out.

But I do want to insert an important note of caution: your energy will not be the same every day, so flexibility is critical. You will want to be aware of what's enough and what's too much as you add or subtract activities and exploration. The idea with your Chapter X is to create the life you value most. It isn't a competition, and nobody's going to give you a prize for stuffing the most into your day. It's a matter of finding balance. If you are the prototypical Type A personality, modifying your urges and tendencies will require determination and a significant amount of self-control. That being said, you would not have been as successful as you were, if you didn't have the discipline.

To build your new life of balance, self-awareness will be key to mindfully being aware when you defer to autopilot and old, ingrained habits. So, let's go back to the blueprint you're creating. This is a great time to revisit your "Values" worksheet and focus on the values that resonate with who you are. If you haven't started thinking about how you will use the time available until your expiration date, now is the time to begin to imagine what activities or actions align with those values. Prioritize the ones that matter most and then let everything else find its proper place.

For example, if you value "helping others," you might explore volunteering or mentorship opportunities. How can you share your knowledge, wisdom, and experience with others? Suppose you value "Joyfulness" and you don't know what that might include. In that case, you have a wide-open vista to explore: travel, art, music, hiking, writing, spending time with family and friends, learning a language, taking a college course, teaching, literally anything that spurs an atom of interest. I've heard men talk about their bucket list of things to do, from skydiving to an African Safari, and from running a marathon to taking an art class in Paris. The good news is that whatever you try, the results, if they're not for you, are of zero consequence. You don't have an upset boss, disappointed clients, or sick patients to deal with. You can't get fired from retirement. You lose nothing by trying something, and the possibility of gain is enormous (not to mention fun); imagine if that rule applied during your work life?

The key here is to align your time with what gives you meaning and purpose on a completely individual basis. I spoke to a friend who decided he wanted to work at his gym, handing out towels. Now, let me be clear, he didn't do it for money; he did it because he enjoyed the camaraderie of the place and enjoyed the interaction with the people. The money he earned probably didn't cover his coffee budget for the week, but he was surprisingly criticized by someone he knows who couldn't believe he would work for minimum wage. Even though he tried to explain that it had nothing to do with the money, his friend insisted he would never do such a thing. Honestly, his friend didn't get it. Joy is joy!

Once you create your purpose and your boundaries that align with your values, you're ready to explore, test, try, experiment, and dip your toe into whatever you can conceive. While you flesh out your blueprint, recognize that several things could happen. You might wake up one morning and feel like your involvement in a particular experience is over—and that is perfectly fine. You are not signing a contract or commitment to keep doing something that no longer makes you happy or feels satisfying. You might also have a temporary or permanent situation that doesn't allow the continuation of your plans, like a physical restriction. While this is not a happy thought, it happens. That's why flexibility is so important in your Chapter X; you want to be prepared with a plan B.

I have a friend who is now in his late 80s. He's been a downhill skier forever. But now he finds it physically too much and has instead turned his attention to cross-country skiing and indoor ice skating. Reality can be a punch in the mouth, especially if you haven't accounted for the fact that, in aging, physical challenges will crop up. But you have a lifetime of experiences dealing with challenges, so you'll be ready to handle this too. Right?

There's a call to action here: curate your life with care. There will be days when you are bursting with energy and days when the call of the couch is screaming. Your body will tell the tale and lead the dance, not your lying brain. One of the big challenges is that you're allowed to take your foot off the gas. You don't have to live the same frantic pace that was your life since you started working. It doesn't mean you're lazy if you're not cranking 14-hour days.

Personally, regardless of the schedule I've created for the day, if I have a miserable night's sleep or am dealing with allergies or something that is sapping my energy, I modify my day accordingly. I was never an alarm clock guy, but then again, I was never a great sleeper (at least since my college years). I get up when I awaken, typically around 6 a.m. (admittedly an ungodly hour). While I used to get up, shower, dress, and get out the door, I now enter my day with gentleness, taking time to step outside, feel the sun on my face, and savor the first cup of coffee. There's something magical about this time of day, feeling grateful and present to the calmness of the moment, the aroma of my home-roasted coffee, without the "to-do" list shouting in my brain.

Finding balance in your life is the goal. After a lifetime of being restricted by parents, school, work, and family, you're being released into the "wild," and it takes time to acclimate. The right amount of activity, the right amount of rest, the right amount of intellectual stimulation, etc. But there is no recipe like baking a cake. You must find your own level of what you need and want, considering the inevitability of unexpected changes. It takes a willingness to self-monitor how you feel at the end of the day. If you're stressed or exhausted, perhaps you need to pull back a little. Think of it like a science experiment: add a little more of this, take a little away from that, and see what happens. It's your life, you're in control of what you're in control of. That being said, control is a tricky word. Knowing what you actually control is the key here.

I hope this helps you think about your boundaries and integrating your life so that it flows with the least amount of stress and the most amount of joy. Life balance is a constant challenge of fine-tuning and adjustments, a never-ending practice of refinement.

Meanwhile, embrace the experience of change, growth, and joy in this wonderful next chapter. You've worked a lifetime, and if you have the blessings of financial security, it's your turn to play and experience life in a whole new way.

"What Are You Retiring To?" by Robert McEachern

A little about my background: I have spent 47 years in financial services and am approaching my retirement from the profession at the end of this month. I am fortunate enough to still be able to pop into the office if desired to assist or do whatever is needed on an unlicensed basis.

I talked to many clients over the past few years from a more holistic point of view. One question I always asked was: "What are you retiring to?" And I continually sought feedback on this to assist in their planning. It was not just about the money, but also about their continued learning, hobbies, community, social outlets, and how they could contribute. I also mentioned that they now had another 40 to 50 hours a week to fill as they desired to. Some clients tuned into this, but many did not, as it was, perhaps, too much of a habit change for them to follow this route. That was their choice, and many did not become clients.

I personally started my retirement (if you wanted to call it that) planning about 12 years ago, and am now 72. I chose to cut back my work hours in three or four phases, reducing my time at the office to under 10 hours per week this year. Interestingly enough, I read Michael Kay's column regarding why retiring to play golf may not be suitable for some people. However, I discovered golf four years ago, and it is one of the methods I use to keep fit, in addition to walking, jogging, tai chi, using the treadmill and weight room, and swimming at the pool in the winter.

I also returned to a stamp-collecting hobby that I had left 40 years ago, and now have a network of new friends in that area. I have brought on new friends who are like-minded and of a more positive nature than some I had in the past, and also some who, like me, feel they are "super agers." My mother is one of these at 95, still driving, volunteering, and living on her own, with 18 great-grandchildren to help keep her young. Grandchildren have the power to do so, and my mother is a great role model for me.

I also started learning French (my worst high school subject) earlier this year, so I can converse in French with my two grandchildren who speak it. I firmly believe that if the brain— or body, for that matter—is not kept active, you lose many faculties. I now see that my friends my age have no plan for living their lives on purpose, but rather by default, which means their health and health span will suffer. I feel very fortunate to have adopted this outlook on living my life by design and to regularly follow those who share a similar attitude. I will continue to give back and keep a positive outlook when I can.

. . . .

CHAPTER 11

There Will Be Challenges

"Challenges are what make life interesting;
overcoming them is what makes life
meaningful."

—*Joshua J. Marine, author and magician*

But before you leap away, tossing flower petals and singing the "Hallelujah" chorus, I must pull back on the reins just a bit to provide some framing. You need to consider that pretty much everything you're used to is going to change. We've gone over some of these things earlier in the book, but let's spell them out. You're going to have to come to terms with:

1. The fact that change is uncomfortable.
2. The fact that your identity as a person *will* change.
3. The fact that what you spent your life doing is over.
4. The fact that this next chapter inevitably ends in death.
5. The idea that the runway is short and the challenges significant (decline in physical and possibly mental capacities) is concerning. Remember, you're healthy until you're not.

6. The fact that relationships will change . . . after a lifetime of "going" to work, you're now with your spouse 24/7; or find yourself without a partner (more about this in the next chapter).

7. Your social structure is shifting; some things might have to be recreated.

8. Shifting thoughts on what meaning and purpose really means to you.

9. Redefining time and how it is used.

10. Reintroducing the idea of *fun*.

11. Channeling your "competitive nature" into new, productive directions.

OK, so these feel big, onerous, scary, terrible, and not fun. But we're going to dig deeper on these things, so don't get crazy. Let me assure you, again and again, *you've got this*. Remember, you're a novice at this whole retirement thing, so don't forget the whole elephant eating thing . . . it's one bite at a time, and patience is necessary, if not entirely welcome. Just because something is new and different doesn't make it bad. Remember, too, we're starting with joyful erasure of the responsibilities, schedules, demands, pressures, and frustrations of work. There's this big shiny gold ring for you to grab hold of on this merry-go-round ride of life. So go for it! All you must do is just stay on the ride.

But to stay in the proverbial saddle, you have to engage the tools we discussed in Part 2, like groundedness. If you are firmly grounded—which is a good thing and very different from being "planted," which is not a good thing—you can access the possibilities that await. For example, you might be dealing with a hip or knee that's been cranky for years, and the orthopedist has been telling you that a replacement is on the horizon. Armed with that information, you might want to determine what kind of physical activity is best for your particular situation. Just be realistic about it. I would think that mogul skiing is probably not in your best interest. That's what I mean by groundedness. Be sensible about boundaries. Know where you are, what you can do, and what is appropriate. I'd say the same thing applies when making large expenditures that take you outside of your safe spending amount. "Knowledge is good." (Can you name the movie?)

Getting back to the list of preceding challenges, let's start with my favorite: change is uncomfortable. Duh! Yes, it's uncomfortable for a reason; I talked about your caveman brain earlier. I'm not expecting you to skip joyfully into the thorny nettles of change, but if you recall from the exercises, you've done it a *billion* times already. You've ventured into terra incognita many times, and you'd think your lizard brain would have gotten over it by now, but no. It will continue to push you into stasis until your last breath. Sorry. I suggest that when the resistance begins to stir, you use it to ask important questions, such as: "What am I resisting?" and "How can I positively channel this?" and "What am I afraid of?"

I don't know about you, but I remember, as a young child, that there was a monster in the closet just waiting for me to close my eyes at night so it could spring out and devour me. The antidote, of course, was to bust open the door and see that there was no monster, just your annoying younger brother snoring in the next room. We need to recognize our resistance points and push the door open. I don't know whether I should let you in on the big secret . . . but because we are on this amazing journey together, I will. Ready? Change will come fast and furious from here on out, and because you're not working crazy hours and immersed in your career, you'll now have more time and space to notice. Oh, well . . . .

Let's move on to the battle over identity. We've talked about this one before. It's a big one for many men. One way out of this mindset might be to replace your identity with a new one. Instead of "I am a doctor," you might replace it with "I am a learner," "I am a seeker of new experiences," or "I am focused on devoting quality time with my grandchildren." A brief warning here: once you are no longer your title, chances are pretty good that you will imagine the judgment coming from others. Whether it's true or not doesn't mean a thing. By now, you know that what other people think is none of your business. Good news: you get to create the supporting phrase that aligns with who you aspire to become, and those who sit in judgment can go pound sand.

Coming to terms with the fact that a massive chapter in your life is now over is another obstacle that might need acknowledging. For me, this was huge. I was so focused on creating my next chapter that I failed to recognize the "death" of my previous life and the firm I had created. I just didn't see it coming, but it slammed me into a depression, nonetheless. I needed to grieve, to acknowledge that something I created from nothing, but a vision was now gone, over, kaput, done, *finito*. Even though I knew in my heart that the firm and the clients were in great hands with my partner, my feelings went much deeper. I needed time to understand what was going on in my body and what it was that had put me in such a terrible state.

Once I realized what was attacking my usually optimistic persona, I was able to begin reframing my feelings by celebrating what I had built, the people I had helped, and the colleagues I had hired and nurtured. This grieving and reflection process was immensely healing, and after it was over, I was able to shift my thinking in a positive light. "Now that I am no longer responsible for running my firm, I now have the opportunity to explore . . . ."

The idea of the inevitability of death is always out there. We don't see it while we're young, unless we've experienced traumatic incidents like the death of a spouse, or parent, or loved one, or the fragility of life. But this stage of life, when the runway is a lot shorter, is like one of Sergio Leone's distinctive super zoom-ins. But instead of an action scene, it's an extreme close-up montage of your current life stage and challenges, things that you've been too distracted by the immediacy of life to really examine until now. Like, how does the hair in my nose and ears grow like weeds? But it's here, and while the thought of aging and decrepitude is less than something to do cartwheels over, what could be a better call-to-action to live with gratitude, focus on what's important (remember your work on isolating your values), and use your time in a way that reflects the person you described in your previously created eulogies.

Whether you are married, partnered, or live alone, the chances are that the relationships in your life will change. You need to prepare yourself for this. If you are married or partnered, it is vital that you and your significant other engage in conversations about expectations and how your new schedule will impact the other. If your spouse is used to you being at work from 7 a.m. to 7 p.m. and now you're home 24/7, rest assured, you will be disrupting their routine. This is most certainly an elephant-eating exercise. I suggest making the conversations short, focused, and open. Talk about expectations and boundaries. Share your vision and your concerns. Elicit full and open responses. If the going gets tough, consider doing some counseling together. I've witnessed the negative impact on couples who hadn't come to terms with this life shift and how it affected their lives together.

Many years ago, I had a client who, on his retirement, was really enjoying being home. His wife, who had her own routine, became increasingly frustrated by his constant micro-managing and interruptions. At one of our meetings, she was at her wit's end, threatening to kill him and then me if I didn't help him figure out how to get out of the house and out of her business.

While she smiled when she made her statement, I wasn't going to ignore her.

Relatedly, the shift into Chapter X also impacts your social connections, work friends, and those in your daily orbit while you're still working. You're no longer part of the team, no longer in the know, no longer . . . relevant? You know those performers who pull tablecloths out from under the dinnerware? Well, it's kind of like that . . . the tablecloth has been yanked out from under you, and those remaining are still standing while you've been whisked away. It can be, to say the least, destabilizing. You will have to put on your big boy pants and discover who's on your team and who's not, and then start working to build a new team, if necessary.

Building new friendships can be daunting, especially if you're a bit of an introvert. But don't get depressed about it. Here's where having that explorer mentality, that curiosity muscle, is so important. Just imagine, the classes, the gym, the golf course, the pickleball or tennis court, the affinity groups, the hiking club, the synagogue or church, the park, the coffee shop, the MeetUp groups, you name it, wherever there are people, you have an opportunity to connect and create new relationships.

Besides the opportunity of creating a new tribe, you also have time to reconnect with old friends. OK, sure, you haven't seen these people since high school and you have nothing in common with them now—but actually, you had a friendship with them for a reason, way back when, and you have no idea what's happened since then. Reconnection is an excellent gift if you take the opportunity to put yourself out there. Let me remind you, once again, there is *nothing* at stake. If it works, great. If it doesn't blossom, you certainly are not in any way diminished. Everything about this period of life should be geared toward exploration. Creating a social net is vital to your mental health and overall happiness. More will be added about this in the next chapter.

After a lifetime of focusing on your career and raising a family, this chapter is a book of empty pages waiting to be filled with new ideas, new purpose, and redefinitions of what things provide meaning. Too many men find themselves stumbling over the definition of *meaning* and *purpose*, as if there was a hidden definition that needed to be lived up to. Let me say this as indelicately as possible: it's a load of crap!

The reason for this false thinking is that after a lifetime of work where you were defined by certain particular standards of success, you're now in the space where no such standards exist. It's you, your imagination, your values, and your courage to explore your way toward what is meaningful and purposeful to *you*! It's just that simple, if you'll excuse my use of the word *simple*.

My wife and I were having dinner with my cousin and her husband, who is a retired executive from Big Pharma. He lived his life knowing that his career could be cut short at any time due to the eccentricities of an industry that was rife with mergers, changes, and workforce cuts. He survived all the changes and retired. He has devoted time to home projects and hiking. Then he pivoted to focusing on vacation planning. He devotes time to investigating, exploring, and comparing travel opportunities, and guess what . . . he loves it! He doesn't have to pass anyone's judgment about it. He is doing what he loves. Bravo!

For me, meaning and purpose vary with the day and how I am feeling. For example, if I am energetic, a purposeful day will include rigorous exercise and recovery time. If I have some time with my family, that also checks the box of meaningful. If I am not feeling very energetic, a purposeful day will include rest, reading, and light activity, maybe a lunch or coffee with a friend. There's nothing lofty; I haven't cured cancer (nor am I likely to) or solved the issue of world peace. However, for a day to have purpose and meaning, it must contain activities that align with my values. Without that, the day is wasted, a failure!

During our monthly Chapter X group Zoom meetings, I hear a lot of different definitions of *meaning* and *purpose*. Some volunteer as a centerpiece of their week; others write, learn, engage in art, enjoy music, golf, travel, spend time with children and grandchildren, connect with friends, build furniture, work part-time, devote time to rehabbing injuries, exercise—you name it. The point is, it's all meaningful and purposeful to *them*! They define what's meaningful and purposeful.

Are you still looking for help on this front? To figure it out, start by breaking down this obstacle into smaller bites (remember the elephant). Start with your current definitions of *meaning* and *purpose*. Are they your definitions or someone else's? Are they global in scope or local?

Most importantly, do they sound like you and align with your values? The key is to create a structure (and who doesn't like a good structure?) where you have the freedom to test, taste, explore, and try different activities that resonate with who you are on a cellular level. It's a process of discovery; time and patience are required. But in time, these efforts will help you define what's meaningful and purposeful in your life.

Having just mentioned time, isn't it an interesting concept? When you're engaged in something you love, time doesn't even exist. It's that flow state that we all crave. If you've never read *Flow: The Psychology of Optimal Experience* by Mihaly Csikszentmihaly, definitely read it (or reread it). *Flow* is that state of concentration so focused that you're totally absorbed in the activity. While this is the ideal, it is not something you can pull off of a shelf at Target. It requires finding what moves you deeply.

Speaking of time, there's a massive misconception about using time in retirement. I've heard from hundreds of men telling me that they won't be able to fill their days in retirement the same way as when they were working; therefore, they conclude, they'll keep working. I can't think of a more wrong-headed belief. The fact is, you don't have to be engaged in focused activity for 10, 12, or 14 hours a day every day. I don't know about you, but I've pulled all-nighters on out-of-town audits, 18-hour days during tax season, countless hours working on financial plans in the small hours, and, honestly, I don't miss any aspect of it.

I value the quiet time of sitting on my patio with the first cup of coffee of the day. I enjoy walking in the woods or around my neighborhood, listening to the birds, music, or just my thoughts. I relish the time devoted to self-care and a leisurely lunch with a friend. The idea that you need to fill up every minute of every day with activity is missing the point. Retirement is the time to pull back from decades of striving and to channel your remaining time into endeavors that don't necessarily involve work. You can choose to continue your life at a balls-to-the-wall pace, but why? Are you living a story that you've convinced yourself is true?

Let me put this as indelicately as possible: **you are going to die!** Your life will come to an inglorious end, and if all you have at the end is a eulogy of how hard you worked your entire life, you might have missed the point. If you are blessed with financial security, then working until you exit in a horizontal position by choice demands some pretty deep scrutiny. I've heard too many men tell me that they will never retire. I nod my head, "OK." But I know in my heart their statement comes not from a hot burning passion to continue working, but because they just haven't allowed themselves to explore alternatives, to reimagine their life differently. It's the caveman afraid to leave his cave all over again. Those old berries must have fermented, and they're a little loopy.

If you're reading this and still insist your exit will be a horizontal one, I encourage you to visit a local nursing home to see what awaits when you reach decrepitude. Then let's talk. If you're still there, then I salute you and your mission.

Now that I've provided a sufficient amount of attitude adjustment (sometimes, it takes a 2×4 to the head), let's talk about fun. The first thing you need to know is that fun is not a four-letter word. Get it? Somewhere in your upbringing, you received a message that as an adult, your only mission was to work, provide, create wealth, take care of your family, and then die. Well, if you don't mind my saying so, that is pretty %&@$ (think four-letter word) messed up. Is it the message that play was for children? Is it the idea that we leave the fantasy behind us when we pick up the mantle of adulthood?

Whatever the reason, it's another load of crap. Think about the standard bell-shaped curve as a track of our lives. There are stages of development and growth, then a plateau, and then decline. That's kind of our lifecycle, if we're blessed enough to reach this time of life. While I am not particularly religious, I can't help but think of the verse from the Old Testament, "To everything there is a season, and a time to every purpose under heaven." You might even remember the song "Turn, Turn, Turn" by the Byrds. So, if there's a time to work, there's pretty much going to have to be a time to do something else.

I'm sure you can name those who didn't make it this far! While this back-end part of the curve is a gradual slope down, it is within this phase that we have the ability, the time, and indeed the right to reclaim a part of ourselves that we haven't touched since childhood—a wide-open vista of wonder, of curiosity, of activity that brings us joy.

There are barriers for some who enter this stage. For some, it might simply be the belief that they don't deserve it, that they don't know *how* to do it (remember the whole novice to mastery thing?), or other excuses or self-imposed obstacles. Yes, engaging in activities that are fun is different from how you've operated all these decades, but it doesn't make it wrong or bad. Fun is, well, fun! Guess what? You get to determine what that is. But you want to let go of the idea of mastery, especially in the beginning.

Just because you stink at something doesn't mean you can't have fun doing it. The mere process of doing, engaging, learning, and experiencing is the key—not the mastery. Sure, everyone wants to produce Picasso-level art, but *really*? Sure, everyone wants to play guitar like Jimmy Page or drums like Dave Grohl, but *really*? Yes, you're used to being an icon in your field of endeavor, but do you really need that type of glory now? It's time to kick back and enjoy the journey and test, try, explore, laugh, and open your mind to new experiences. I want you to be able to say, "Wow, that was fun!" It's your right and privilege after all the hard work you've done throughout your life.

One of my friends, a retiring attorney, plays guitar with a group of guys. They get together several times a month and play at one of the members' homes. They've been getting together for years. Just having fun playing music. They're not looking to play the Garden, but in their minds, they are transformed when they pick up their instruments. It's wonderful!

The last obstacle I am going to explore is the idea of channeling your competitive nature. Yeah, I bet you still have it. If you didn't have a competitive nature, you'd probably not have been as successful as you are. Like most things, it's a double-edged sword. Being competitive, on the positive side, provides motivation to improve, resilience and grit, clarity and focus, a high level of performance, and lots of energy. But the other side of that blade lies the harmful or dangerous aspects, such as stress and burnout, damage to relationships, perfectionism and fear of failure, loss of enjoyment, and the comparison trap.

I love that you channel your competitive nature into that resilience and grit and the motivation to improve that have taken you so far in life. But on the flip side, the comparison trap, along with the loss of enjoyment and perfectionism, is an insidious monster lurking in the closet, waiting to mess you up. Devote some time to thinking about how your competitive nature can be your best friend or your worst enemy. Lean into the benefits as you remain vigilant to keep the self-sabotaging monster at bay. That, my friend, is another example of self-awareness.

Our lives, from the time of our first awareness, have been filled with obstacles, big and small. But through them all, you persisted. Keep doing that. Keep identifying obstacles and creating plans for progressing through them. Don't get discouraged if the fix isn't immediate; learning how to overcome a difficulty is all part of the process. And with all the tools at your disposal, I'm confident you'll figure it out.

But if the obstacle leaves you frozen without a pathway forward, never hesitate to call in help from friends, family, or a therapist. Throwing your hands up in defeat is not who you are. I know asking for directions seems impossible, and now that you have GPS, it's no longer necessary, but asking for help when you're stuck is truly important. It isn't a sign of weakness, but of strength. Your friends and allies want to help, and you'd certainly do the same if they asked it of you.

Time to move forward—*strongly*!

A VIEW FROM CHAPTER

"10 Tips for Chapter X" by John Harrison, MEd

1. Don't retire until you are ready.

   a. As your retirement target date approaches, it becomes harder to stick with it and do the job. The tendency is to say, "I don't need this hassle." If the stress or the situation is untenable, then retire; otherwise, make sure you do the math or have a plan to ensure your income outlives you.

2. Stay active mentally and physically.

   a. After you make it through the list of things you "Want to do when I retire," make sure you stay engaged.

      i. Mentally: Create projects, learn something new, volunteer, do puzzles, read, write—you get the picture.

      ii. Physically: Start moving or keep moving. Walk, run, go to the gym, do yoga, try Tai Chi, garden, babysit grandkids. Do anything that requires physical effort.

3. Time is finite.

   a. Don't wait to do the things you want to do. Some things take preparation, like getting in shape to hike the Appalachian Trail. Other things, like booking a flight to visit someone you haven't seen in years, can be done today.

4. Friendship takes effort.

   a. Call someone who comes to mind. Invite a friend to lunch. Have a dinner party. Join a face-to-face social group. Invite someone to do something you enjoy, like fishing, walking, dancing, building, or creating. If you don't hear back, call again. If they can't join you this time, follow up.

b. Show up when asked. Show up when needed without being asked.

c. Embrace your weirdness. Others who don't find your weirdness weird are your people. You have to find your people. It takes effort.

5. Find someone to talk to.

a. A teacher. When the student is ready, the teacher appears. Look for them.

b. A friend. Someone who will tell you what you need to hear and not just agree with you or tell you what you want to hear.

c. A spiritual mentor. We are all going to die. We all know someone who is ill, has cancer, or is struggling with health issues. Be at peace with whatever you believe is going to happen when you die.

6. Create activities that will keep you socially engaged on a regular basis.

a. Go to bible study, join a card-playing group, or find people who enjoy plays. Find a buddy who shares your hobby. Volunteer once a week. Get a part-time job, not for the money, but because it is something you enjoy doing,

7. Break things down into doable chunks.

a. For example, I can't manicure my entire yard in a day, but I can cut it today, do the weed eating tomorrow, and trim the trees and bushes the day after that. Job done.

8. It's OK to say no.

    a. If you need time for yourself.

    b. If you don't feel like doing something.

    c. If that person's negativity drains your positivity or energy.

    d. If you are not physically, emotionally, or spiritually able to do whatever it is.

9. Know your limitations.

    a. We are not as young as we used to be.

    b. We are not as strong as we used to be.

    c. We don't recover as fast as we used to.

    d. Maybe you really can't afford to do the thing you want to do.

10. Find your purpose.

    a. Getting healthy.

    b. Become a mentor.

    c. Help someone in need.

    d. Listen more than you speak.

    e. Get to know your adult kids again.

    f. Spend time with grandchildren.

    g. Be creative.

    h. Let go of resentments. It hurts you more than the person or thing you resent.

    i. Learn how to be present. Look people in the eye. Listen intently and intentionally. Put away the phone during conversations. Let the phone ring. Turn off the TV during dinner. When you are with someone, they are the only thing that matters.

j. In a world in which you can be anything, be kind.

11. Bonus Tip:

a. In his book *The Electric Kool-Aid Acid Test,* Tom Wolfe wrote a phrase that he attributes to Ken Kesey: "It's your movie." I take this as encouragement for you to see life as a story or movie that you are directing. You are in control of your time now that you are retired. You can shape your life to be the way you want it.

CHAPTER 12

Take Care of Yourself

> "We are exploring together. We are cultivating
> a garden together, backs to the sun.
> The question is a hoe in our hands and we are
> digging beneath the hard and crusty surface
> to the rich humus of our lives."
> —*Parker J. Palmer*, Let Your Life Speak:
> Listening for the Voice of Vocation

OK, call me Captain Obvious, but, honestly, once you enter your Chapter X, without carefully, mindfully, and intentionally taking care of yourself, you are standing at the brink of circling the drain. Get it? Perhaps that comes off as a bit harsh, but I honestly don't think so. Your health, to the extent that you can maintain, control, and improve it, is your golden ticket to everything going forward. Seriously! Think health span, not lifespan.

Ironically, just 30 minutes before I sat down to write this chapter, I met a man at the pharmacy. I heard him talk to the pharmacist about being retired. As we both left the store, I naturally engaged him and asked how retirement was going for him. I always wonder in these moments whether I will hear a happy story. In this case, he shared that he had retired because he had been diagnosed with pancreatic cancer and was undergoing experimental treatment. He said that he was generally feeling good, was getting anxious to "do something," and wanted to be engaged, productive, and find something meaningful. I rest my case!

Here's a guy who was two or three years from retiring, according to *his* plan, but life had other designs on him. There wasn't a thing he could have done to change the situation; it was just how life presented itself to him. How about you? Do you have a choice, or are you just going to fold your tent and steal away into the night? Remember, you're healthy—until you're not!

Three main areas need your focus. The first is your medical situation. If you're not going for regular checkups and seeking advice when appropriate, you're playing Russian roulette. The second is your emotional health. I've said it before, mental health problems, including depression and suicide, are rampant among retired men. The third area is navigating your body physically. In other words, figuring out what types of exercise are vitally important as you age, and which ones to be cautious about as you get older.

There is a powerful connection between our physical health and our emotional/mental well-being. If you are feeling stress or anxiety, your body will respond with muscle tightness, headaches, and an increased heart rate. If you're feeling sad, your body might respond with feelings of fatigue, low immune function, and sleep disruption. Conversely, if you are feeling love, optimism, or joy, your immune system will be boosted and your cardiovascular system will improve.

Conversely, scientific research has well documented how your body influences your mind. For example, exercise releases endorphins, reduces inflammation, and enhances mood. Good nutrition and good sleep contribute to a positive picture, whereas the opposite (bad diet and poor quality sleep) degrades your mental well-being.

As we're on the subject of sleep, I have to tell you, I am a complete sleep nerd. I've done extensive reading and put in a great deal of effort to achieve the best sleep possible. For example, I use the Oura Ring to track my sleep metrics, including the amount of deep and REM sleep I get as well as my sleep's restfulness and duration. In the evenings, I curate my bedtime routine, reduce screen time, avoid bright lights, and take several supplements aimed at good sleep. My alcohol and my caffeine consumption are also carefully curated, along with the time of day I eat my last meal (heavy digestion can wreak havoc on your sleep cycle). To me, sleep is the key to my day, my energy, and my state of mind.

OK, enough of the high-level stuff. It's time to introduce you to the experts. The following three chapters in the book are contributions from three authorities in their fields. First up is Dr. David Bernstein, a retired geriatrician and the author of several book on health and aging, including *I've Got Some Good News and Some Bad News: You're Old: Tales of a Geriatrician*, *What to Expect in Your 60's, 70's, 80's, and Beyond* and *The Power of Five: The Ultimate Formula for Longevity & Remaining Youthful*.

In addition, Philip Pape, a trainer and nutrition expert, also joined me for a podcast conversation. Nothing replaces knowing what to do and what to avoid. We can get overwhelmed with social media "experts" shouting contradictory messages. I defer to common sense and science-based information.

Last, I have invited one of my podcast guests, Glenn Berger, PhD, LCSW, to offer his thoughts on mental health issues and aging. He is an experienced therapist who is deeply committed to helping people. His guidance is invaluable in honing your self-awareness when challenges rear their ugly head.

You don't need me to tell you how important health is to living your best life. But I couldn't end this chapter without putting it in black and white. You've heard or witnessed enough stories of heart attacks, cancer, dementia, depression, broken body parts, and so on to know the impact these things have on lives and well-being. Last year, for no apparent reason, I came down with a shoulder issue that started in my bicep and ran into my right shoulder. I relentlessly engaged in physical therapy; meanwhile, my ability to work out was significantly impacted. I was *not* a happy camper. I went from 65-pound dumbbell rows to 5 pounds, from 275-pound deadlifts to 70 pounds. Not only was I physically less capable, but I could easily see how my mental state was impacted, too. Thankfully, with the support of the physical therapist and my trainer, I was able to eliminate the problem and resume full-bore exercise.

By the way, my experience is a great example of the mind/body connection on full display. While I was physically limited, my mood was off, my sleep was off, and my body felt awful. I know a lot of men who have experienced the challenge of shoulder surgeries, knee and hip replacements, and chronic back issues. Their challenges are significant; the road to healing can be lengthy. Your determination to stay vigilant regarding your physical and emotional states should be a top priority. Remember, you have every reason in the world to focus on your health and well-being. After all, you've just devoted all this time to figuring out your values, thinking of ways to live those values, and focusing on meaning and purpose and joy. Your health and well-being are the foundation on which all those things rest.

. . . .

CHAPTER 13

The Health Dividend: Maximizing Your Well-Being in Retirement

Contributed by Dr. David Bernstein

Introduction: The Unsung Components of Retirement Security

It's the fourth quarter, the game is on the line, and you've just called a crucial timeout. You're ready to strategize for success in the most critical challenge: achieving a vibrant, healthy, and long retirement.

As an internist specializing in geriatric medicine, I've spent my career helping patients navigate the "fourth quarter" of their lives. Like a dedicated coach, I've guided them to protect their lead or strategically recover from setbacks, always with the goal of a fulfilling retirement ahead.

Aging and retirement present unique challenges, and while financial assets are undeniably important, they simply don't compare to the value of robust health and well-being. A truly successful retirement hinges on lifelong planning and proactive health management.

I observed my father and countless aging patients/adults with significant financial assets whose deteriorated health prevented them from enjoying the opportunities to spend their hard-earned assets. When your body is falling apart, it is hard to spend your fortune.

With a limited number of geriatricians available globally, a proactive approach is essential. This means building a helpful team of medical professionals—physicians, physician assistants, nurse practitioners, gerontologists, and social workers—and working with coaches. This collaborative effort is key to maintaining that fourth-quarter lead or overcoming health deficits, ultimately improving your health trajectory as you age in retirement.

Section 1: "Landmines"—Common Health Obstacles in Life and Retirement

There are five foundational elements I frequently emphasize for promoting health and wellness, and it's never too early—or too late—to incorporate them into your life strategy. For retirees who haven't yet, now is the opportune moment. I call this approach the **Power of 5: five impactful S words** that foster good health and actively reduce chronic inflammation, a major contributor to aging and frailty. These are **Sweets, Sweat, Stress, Sleep, and Sex/Socialization.** While many endorse these concepts, I've chosen these specific S words for their memorable resonance and ease of integration into a lifelong health plan.

I. Manage **Sweets**—if you haven't already, explore healthy eating lifestyles and choose the one that suits you best. I highly endorse a Mediterranean eating lifestyle for several reasons:

   a) The enjoyment of eating fresh foods, especially plant-based.

   b) Its use of healthy grains and less processed products.

c) For many years, it has been recognized as the best eating style for weight management as well as for cardiovascular, brain, and overall health.

d) It offers flexibility that most people can adapt to, eating healthy fish, poultry, and limited amounts of red meat. It advocates for the consumption of lots of fresh fruits, vegetables, whole grains, beans, and seeds.

2. Incorporate movement/exercise/**Sweat** into daily life, as otherwise inactivity and a sedentary lifestyle take a powerful physical and mental toll. Incorporating even 30 minutes of daily movement or exercise can profoundly impact your health and overall fitness. It's a powerful antidote to a sedentary lifestyle.

3. Manage **Stress**—retirement is a time to adjust to a life with far less stress and more time for enjoyable activities. In our hectic lives, we may have never learned how to de-stress; now is the time. Incorporating activities such as meditation and other forms of relaxation reduces the release of harmful hormones in our bodies, thereby reducing inflammation and its negative consequences.

4. Improve **Sleep**—until the past few decades, there was little emphasis on sleep in the medical world, and it was typically not given enough attention in our busy preretirement lives. Yet, 7 to 8 hours of quality sleep is crucial to healthy aging, avoiding cognitive decline and managing stress, inflammation, and obesity.

5. **Socialization**—we are only beginning to understand how important having relationships is to healthy aging. After 40 or 50 years of working day in and day out, we will all benefit from learning how to forge and maintain healthy relationships.

Address Unmanaged Chronic Conditions: I cannot stress enough the importance of regular medical checkups and adherence to medical advice from medical professionals to manage deadly chronic medical conditions such as high blood pressure, diabetes, elevated cholesterol, overweight and obesity—and these are but a few of the conditions that shorten life expectancy. Waiting until retirement to address and manage these and other medical conditions will absolutely spoil retirement. Neglecting this aspect of retirement planning guarantees more frequent and often urgent appointments with medical professionals, which can quickly consume your precious retirement time. Proactive management of conditions like high blood pressure, diabetes, elevated cholesterol, and obesity is paramount for extending both your lifespan and your "health span"—the years you can truly enjoy.

Avoid exposures to these risk factors that contribute to cognitive decline. Introduction to the "Big 13": I've never met anyone who looked forward to experiencing cognitive decline or dementia in retirement. The good news is that becoming familiar with the 13 primary cognition-related risk factors, and addressing them proactively, even well before retirement, significantly increases the likelihood of preventing or delaying cognitive decline. We'll delve into this crucial topic in Section 3 that follows.

Section 2: The "Mindset" Shift—Embracing Proactive Health Management

Concept: Retirement isn't just a financial transition; it's a profound shift in mindset. While developing a solid financial plan is paramount, it's equally crucial to embrace the psychological and pragmatic aspects of health planning. This section explores key mindsets vital for a truly vibrant retirement.

Key Mindsets to Foster:

- **Investment in Self:** Framing health as an ongoing investment, much like financial planning, is incredibly important but often overlooked. One ought to consider how enjoyable retirement will be for the person who sacrificed his physical health only to find himself handicapped and unable to engage in all that he has dreamt about and saved for. Think of people who worked in noisy environments and did not shield their ears, or those who failed to wear protective eyewear or clothes, and experienced permanent discomfort or impairment as a result. My uncle was a carpet layer, and when he reached retirement age, he was incapacitated because of the hard labor he had performed.

- **Proactive vs. Reactive:** Shifting from waiting for health problems to emerge to actively preventing them is a game-changer. A proactive approach dramatically reduces your disease burden, delays or avoids serious complications, and, ultimately, means fewer disruptive trips to medical professionals during your hard-earned retirement years.

- **Holistic View of Health:** Recognizing the interconnectedness of physical, mental, and social well-being is fundamental to successful aging. Studies consistently show that a holistic approach—like the Power of 5 S's discussed previously—adopted early in life or at the time of retirement, significantly adds years of health and enjoyment. Embrace this integrated view.

- **Adaptability:** The ability to adjust to physical changes and seek support is another component that will lead to better health in retirement. Just as with making course corrections to a financial plan when there are changes in the market or events in life, happy or sad, adaptability is essential. An unexpected health issue may lead to lifestyle changes that require careful consideration.

Section 3: "Tools" to Address Health in Retirement—A Geriatrician's Playbook

Concept: Just as a winning sports team needs a well-rehearsed playbook, a successful, healthy retirement requires a documented plan with clear, actionable steps. My wife and I, in co-authoring our own health journal, find it an invaluable tool for tracking our progress. Whatever tool you choose—be it an app, a planner, or a simple notebook—consult it regularly and commit to the plan you've developed. An accountability partner can also be incredibly beneficial here.

✘ **Regular Medical Check-ups:** Thankfully, healthcare has evolved from merely treating acute conditions to embracing a proactive model of preventive care. For years, I've relied on the recommendations of highly respected sources like The U.S. Preventive Services Task Force, an independent panel of experts in disease prevention and evidence-based medicine. Open and comfortable communication with your trusted medical professionals on all health topics is paramount. Essentially, there are three primary reasons to engage with your healthcare team:

» For the diagnosis of emerging problems or conditions that could become chronic.

» For the ongoing evaluation and management of existing chronic medical conditions like hypertension, diabetes, elevated cholesterol, and heart disease.

» For crucial screenings for preventable diseases such as various cancers (breast, colon, prostate, lung) as well as behavioral health, psychosocial issues, substance abuse, and cognitive decline.

- **Personalized Exercise Plan:** Encouragement of activities that are enjoyable and sustainable. Not everyone can adopt the same plan, and individualization is important. Cardio, balance, and flexibility are important, while strength training and muscle building appear to be essential to healthy aging. These movement activities can reduce fall risk and the downhill progression that often follows in older adults.

- **Nutritional Guidance:** Establish and commit to following balanced eating, including more plant and fewer animal products, and perhaps adopt a Mediterranean-style diet. Consider plant-based protein alternatives, such as tofu, tempeh, and seitan, and add legumes, nuts, and seeds.

- **Social Engagement Strategies:** Social interaction is one of the most important, if not the most important, components in healthy aging, but it does not always come easy—especially to men. Making friends after years of just going to work, coming home, and following the grind is difficult. It takes an intentional approach to make new friends and reestablish previous friendships. Other ways to become involved and meet new people include volunteering, joining clubs, and forming friendships through these encounters.

- **Stress Management Techniques:** Incorporating activities such as mindfulness (a mental state achieved by focusing one's awareness on the present moment, while calmly acknowledging and accepting one's feelings, thoughts, and bodily sensations; used as a therapeutic technique), meditation, hobbies, and spending time in nature. I enjoy getting some sunshine early in my day and tending to my garden. It does not take much for me to feel the effect of connecting to nature. The morning sunlight helps manage my circadian rhythm, helping me fall asleep at night.

✻ **Adequate Sleep Hygiene:** Consistent sleep patterns are imperative to healthy retirement. Shooting for 7–8 hours of nightly quality sleep reduces chronic inflammation, assists in weight control, and reduces the risk for cognitive decline and chronic illnesses. Getting sunlight exposure early in your day is one more way to keep your circadian clock on schedule.

✻ **Special Focus: The "Big 13" Tools for Brain Health— Addressing Cognitive Decline Risk Factors:** Cognitive decline is a profound concern for many as they age, often fueled by witnessing family members or friends experience it, leading to a belief that little hope exists for avoidance or delay. While the concern is valid, the critical truth is that many risk factors for cognitive decline are modifiable. In my 40 years of practice, we haven't seen significant pharmaceutical breakthroughs to stop, slow, or delay the development of dementia in susceptible individuals. This underscores precisely why we must take these modifiable risk factors so seriously.

For each of these 13 items, there are practical "tools" or strategies to mitigate risk:

The "Big 13" Risk Factors Contributing to Cognitive Decline

Here is the complete list of 13 well-established risk factors contributing to cognitive decline, often cited in medical literature (e.g., The Lancet Commission on dementia prevention, intervention, and care). For each of the following, I will cite the risk and provide tools or interventions to mitigate or reduce the risk:

1. **Less Education:** Lower levels of education in early life are associated with a higher risk of cognitive decline in later life.

   » **Tool:** Lifelong learning, engaging in intellectually stimulating activities, learning new skills or languages in retirement.

2. **Hypertension (Midlife):** High blood pressure, particularly in middle age, significantly increases the risk of later-life dementia.

   » **Tool:** Regular blood pressure monitoring, adherence to prescribed medications, adopting a heart-healthy diet (e.g., DASH diet or Mediterranean), and regular exercise.

3. **Obesity (Midlife):** Being overweight or obese in middle age is linked to an elevated risk of cognitive impairment.

   » **Tool:** Maintaining a healthy weight through balanced nutrition and regular physical activity.

4. **Hearing Impairment:** Untreated hearing loss is a significant and modifiable risk factor for cognitive decline.

   » **Tool:** Regular hearing checks, use of hearing aids if recommended, and addressing underlying causes of hearing loss.

5. **Traumatic Brain Injury (TBI):** A history of moderate or severe TBI can increase the risk of dementia.

   » **Tool:** Practicing head safety (e.g., wearing helmets for cycling, seatbelts in cars), preventing falls, and avoiding ladders after age 65.

6. **Alcohol Consumption (Excessive):** Heavy drinking is neurotoxic and can contribute to cognitive decline.

   » **Tool:** Moderating alcohol intake (e.g., limited to recommended guidelines, or abstaining), seeking support for alcohol use disorder if necessary. There is increasing support for abstinence.

7. **Air Pollution:** Exposure to air pollutants, particularly fine particulate matter, has been linked to increased risk of dementia.

   » **Tool:** Minimizing exposure to polluted areas, using air purifiers indoors, and advocating for cleaner air policies.

8. **Smoking:** Current smoking is a major risk factor for dementia and other chronic diseases.

   » **Tool:** Quitting smoking, seeking support programs for cessation.

9. **Depression:** Depression, especially in later life, is strongly associated with an increased risk of cognitive decline.

   » **Tool:** Seeking professional help for depression (therapy, medication), engaging in enjoyable activities, and maintaining social connections.

10. **Social Isolation:** Lack of social engagement and feelings of loneliness are detrimental to brain health.

» **Tool:** Maintaining strong social networks, joining clubs, volunteering, and engaging in community activities.

11. **Physical Inactivity:** A sedentary lifestyle is a significant contributor to cognitive decline.

» **Tool:** Engaging in regular physical activity (aerobic, strength, balance), aiming for at least 150 minutes of moderate-intensity exercise per week.

12. **Diabetes:** Type 2 diabetes increases the risk of dementia.

» **Tool:** Managing blood sugar levels through diet, exercise, and medication, with regular monitoring. Some of the newer medications seem to have longevity benefits.

13. **Diet (Unhealthy/Poor Nutrition):** Diets high in saturated fats, processed foods, and sugar, and low in fruits, vegetables, and whole grains, can negatively affect brain health.

» **Tool:** Adopting a brain-healthy diet such as the Mediterranean diet or MIND diet, focusing on whole foods and plant-based

Section 4: Conclusion—Your Health, Your Legacy

* **Reiterate:** There is a profound connection between health and a fulfilling retirement. Many contemplate their legacy and, in retirement, realize that it was not the work they did but the family they raised, the friends they had, and the things they accomplished both personally and in their community. Only by enjoying good health can this part of life and legacy be achieved.

- ✴ **Empowerment:** Readers are encouraged to take ownership of their health journey; in the end, finances, family, and health are what truly matter. Start as early as possible to take inventory; set and follow a plan for the best health possible.

- ✴ **Call to Action:** Engage family and friends, collaborate with your healthcare team, and integrate health planning into your overall retirement strategy.

David Bernstein, MD, is an award-winning physician and author who is board-certified in both internal medicine and geriatrics. His 40 years of experience have provided him with opportunities to observe and empathize with thousands of adults as they age. He has integrated his experience in practice and developed a strategy to enhance longevity and vitality. Connect with David at PowerOf5Life.com.

CHAPTER 14

. . . .

Aging Backward

Contributed by Philip Pape

The email arrived on a Monday evening, and the subject line was simple: "I need help."

It was from a podcast listener named Jim, and he wrote:

I don't even know where to start. I'm a 50-something guy, sitting here at 330 pounds, and I feel like my body has been fighting against me for years. No matter what I do, the weight just doesn't come off. I've tried eating "clean," cutting carbs, walking, you name it . . . and all I've gotten is more frustrated and exhausted.

I'm scared about where my health is headed. My joints ache, my energy is gone, and every time I look in the mirror, I feel like I've already lost the battle. I want to believe it's not too late, but I honestly don't know what to do anymore.

Can you help someone like me? Or am I just too far gone?

I stared at those words for several minutes. Jim wasn't just describing his weight. He was expressing his fear of being beyond help, beyond hope, beyond redemption. He was describing what happens when we mistake temporary setbacks for permanent failure.

One year later, Jim had lost 60 pounds, dropping from 330 to 270. He could deadlift 405 pounds. This is from a man who had been completely sedentary just 12 months earlier. His body fat had dropped by 13%. His resting heart rate fell from over 80 beats per minute to under 60.

His blood work told an even more dramatic story. His A1C dropped from 7.2% to 5.4%, his LDL cholesterol fell from 165 to 98 mg/dL, and his triglyceride levels decreased significantly from 280 to 120 mg/dL.

Although we're going to talk more about why lifting weights was the foundation of Jim's seemingly unreal success, the real victory wasn't the weight he lifted. It was the weight he now refused to carry any longer: the weight of accepting that he was "too far gone."

What happened between that desperate email and that remarkable transformation reveals something profound about the nature of aging itself, and our power to rewrite its rules.

The Myth

In 1961, Leonard Hayflick made a discovery that would haunt biology for decades. Working with human cells in his laboratory, he found that they could only divide a finite number of times before dying—52 divisions, then death. The Hayflick limit, as it came to be known, seemed to prove that aging was programmed into our very DNA.

For years, this discovery reinforced what many already believed: that decline was inevitable, that our bodies were ticking time bombs, that growing older meant growing weaker. The research seemed to confirm our worst fears about aging.

But Hayflick was studying cells in petri dishes, not bodies in motion.

Herman Pontzer, an evolutionary anthropologist at Duke University, suspected that something was amiss with our understanding of aging and metabolism. In 2021, he published a study in *Science*[10] that would overturn decades of assumptions. Using doubly labeled water (the gold standard method where water molecules are labeled with stable isotopes to measure energy expenditure), he tracked the metabolic rates of 6,421 people across 29 countries, ranging from infants to centenarians.

What he found was startling.

When adjusted for body size and muscle mass, total energy expenditure remained stable from age 20 to 60. Not declining with age, but completely stable. It was only after 60 that metabolic rate began to drop, and even then, the decline was modest, at about 0.7% per year.

This wasn't supposed to be possible. For decades, we blamed middle-aged weight gain on a slowing metabolism. We attributed fatigue and weakness to biological inevitability. We accepted that our bodies were betraying us.

We were wrong.

The problem wasn't that our engines were failing. The problem was that we'd stopped feeding them fuel. We'd stopped using them.

The Science

Jim's transformation began not with a workout plan or a diet, but with a simple revelation: most of what we call aging is just disuse. Starting around age 30, the average person loses 3% to 8% of their muscle mass per decade, a condition known as *sarcopenia*. By 60,

---

10 Pontzer, H., Yamada, Y., Sagayama, H., et al. "Daily energy expenditure through the human life course." Science. 2021; 373 (6556):808-812. doi: 10.1126/science.abe5017

this accelerates dramatically. But this isn't happening because of birthdays. It's happening because of choices.

Your body operates like a ruthlessly efficient accountant. It looks at your muscle tissue and asks a simple question: "What have you done for me lately?" If the answer is nothing, it starts cutting costs. Muscle is expensive to maintain. It burns calories even at rest, requires a constant intake of protein, and demands energy for repair and maintenance. Why keep it around if you're not using it?

This biological efficiency explains why Jim felt like his body was "fighting against him." Each year of inactivity had cost him muscle. Each pound of muscle lost had slowed his metabolism. Each metabolic slowdown had made weight loss harder. He wasn't lazy, weak, or broken. He was experiencing the predictable consequence of a system designed for survival, not for sitting.

However, there is good news: muscle loss isn't inevitable. Neither is metabolic decline. Neither is the steady accumulation of fat around your waist, the aching joints, the vanishing energy. These are symptoms of disuse, not aging. And disuse has a cure.

When Jim started lifting weights, something remarkable happened not just to his body, but to his biology. His muscles began producing compounds called myokines, molecular messengers that communicate with every organ in the body. These myokines improved Jim's insulin sensitivity, enhanced his fat oxidation, reduced his inflammation, and even supported his brain health.

His muscles had become an endocrine organ, a hormone factory, a pharmacy producing exactly the medicines his body needed.

The research on resistance training reads like science fiction, yet the benefits are all too real. Starting with the obvious, it can increase physical function through more strength and muscle mass. It can help preserve your muscle when losing weight, resulting in a more favorable body fat distribution (in other words, you lose fat, not muscle). It can increase bone density by 1–3% annually, reducing the risk of fractures. It can boost testosterone levels by 15–20% in men over 40. It can improve insulin sensitivity by up to 25%, enhance glucose uptake, and improve lipid profiles, thereby enhancing metabolic health and reducing the risk of Type 2 diabetes and cardiovascular disease. It can reduce visceral fat (the dangerous belly fat around your organs). It can enhance cognitive function and memory, executive function, working memory, and mood.

But wait, there's more. Resistance training can strengthen connective tissues, such as tendons and ligaments, which improves joint stability. It reduces pain and risk in conditions like knee osteoarthritis or lower back pain. It can reduce symptoms of depression and anxiety comparable to some medications. It can give you deeper, more restorative sleep (possibly via improved circadian rhythm regulation and reduced nighttime stress hormones).

And finally, emerging research suggests that resistance training may reduce inflammation and oxidative stress, upregulate mitochondrial biogenesis, and even slow down telomere shortening. All of these are mechanisms linked to healthier aging and longevity.

This isn't about building bigger biceps or impressing people at the gym. This is about reprogramming your physiology down to the cellular level, albeit one rep at a time in the gym.

The Method

Jim started with bodyweight squats in his living room. He could barely manage 10 without gasping for air (let alone get down to proper depth . . . yet). His form was not great. His confidence was worse.

"I felt like a fraud," he told me later. "Like I was pretending to be someone I wasn't."

But pretending is exactly how transformation begins. You act like the person you want to become until you become that person. You lift weights like someone who lifts weights until you become someone who lifts weights. You eat protein like someone who prioritizes protein until protein becomes a priority.

The magic isn't in the complexity (or even intensity), it's in the consistency. Understanding what to be consistent with comes down to three fundamental pillars: how you train, how you fuel your body, and how you recover. Get these right, and transformation becomes not just possible, but inevitable.

Pillar #1: Training

If the goal is to improve how we move our bodies against load (resistance), we should move in a natural human way. In that case, we can start with the fundamental human movement patterns:

- **Squatting** (the bodyweight squat, barbell back squat, goblet squat, and so on)
- **Pulling** (a "pick up and put down" hip hinge like deadlifting, vertical pulling like pull-ups or chin-ups, and horizontal pulling like "row" type movements)
- **Pressing** (both horizontal, like the flat bench press, and vertical, like the shoulder press)

Exercises associated with these patterns are called *compound movements*. They work multiple muscle groups simultaneously (hence "compound"), giving you maximum return on your time. They're also the movements that matter most in real life: getting up from a chair, picking up your grandchildren, carrying groceries, moving furniture.

Those are the movement patterns or exercises, but how do you apply those patterns to get the benefits we discussed earlier?

The key here is *progressive overload*. Each session, you challenge your muscles slightly more than in the previous session. Maybe it's an extra five pounds. Perhaps it's one more rep. Maybe it's an additional set. Your body responds to this progressive challenge by adapting. It builds new muscle fibers (technically, it increases the number and thickness of your *sarcomeres*, the basic unit of muscle contraction). It strengthens existing muscles and improves the efficiency of your nervous system.

This is how Jim went from struggling with bodyweight squats to deadlifting 405 pounds. Not through some miracle program or secret technique. And also not through random "exercise" or "working out." Not by chasing a sweat, "burning fat," or getting sore. Instead, Jim built strength and muscle by training with consistent, progressive loading over time.

But training is only part of the equation. Let's discuss the other two parts.

Pillar #2: Nutrition

Here's where most men over 40 make several mistakes. They focus solely on restricting calories (usually through a well-marketed diet, such as carnivore or keto) or eliminating entire food groups, when what they really need is a strategic and sustainable approach.

Protein is critical (more than you think). As we age, our bodies develop what scientists call "anabolic resistance," a decreased ability to build muscle from the protein we consume. The research is clear: older adults need approximately 0.7 to 1 gram of protein per pound of body weight daily. For a 180-pound man, that's about 125 to 180 grams of protein per day.

Energy balance is still a thing (but it's not about cutting calories). Whether you're trying to lose fat or build muscle, you need to match your energy intake to your goals. This is where the concept of "energy flux" becomes powerful. Rather than eating as little as possible, you want to eat as much as possible while still achieving your body composition goals. This means being active enough to support a higher calorie intake, which provides more nutrients, better recovery, improved performance, and greater adherence to your plan.

Carbohydrates fuel performance (and lots more). Despite decades of carb-phobic messaging, carbohydrates are your muscles' preferred fuel source. When you're lifting weights consistently, adequate carbohydrates ensure you can train with intensity, recover properly, and maintain muscle mass during fat loss phases. Think of carbs as the gasoline for your strength training engine.

Flexible (but controlled) eating beats rigid rules. The most sustainable approach isn't about "clean" or "dirty" foods, it's about finding a way of eating that you can maintain long-term while hitting your protein targets and energy needs. This might mean 80% whole foods and 20% whatever you enjoy. It might mean tracking your intake for a while to learn about your eating patterns, portion sizes, and macro balance. The goal is to develop a system of eating that you can stick to for life and tweak as needed as your goals shift (such as fat loss vs. building muscle).

Back to Jim.

Jim discovered all of this when he started tracking his food intake. He thought he was eating plenty of protein, but he was barely hitting 80 grams per day. When he doubled his protein intake and started eating adequate carbohydrates to fuel his training, everything changed. His recovery improved. His energy stabilized. His cravings disappeared. He felt full and satisfied for the first time in years, despite being in a calorie deficit.

The real breakthrough came when Jim understood that his body wasn't his enemy. It was his partner. It had been trying to protect him all along, storing energy for the famine it thought was coming, preserving resources for the challenges it thought he might face. When he started giving it the signals it needed (resistance training, adequate protein, sufficient energy, and plenty of recovery), it responded rapidly and with enthusiasm.

Pillar #3: Recovery

Sleep, it turns out, is where the transformation occurs. Your workout is the stimulus. Your recovery is the adaptation. Growth hormone pulses through your system. Muscle fibers repair and rebuild. Memories consolidate. The day's stress dissolves.

Jim had been treating sleep like a luxury, something to sacrifice when life got busy. But sleep isn't optional. It's when your body does its most important work. Studies on sleep deprivation show increased cravings (for energy-dense foods), higher visceral fat storage, and suppressed hormones. Therefore, a good night's sleep (both duration and especially quality) isn't a suggestion but a requirement for anyone serious about their health and body composition. Consistent bedtimes and wake times are a great place to start.

Stress management is equally critical. Chronic stress elevates cortisol, which promotes muscle breakdown and fat storage. For Jim, this meant finding time for activities that nourished rather than depleted him. Walks in nature and sunlight. Playing his bagpipes (yes, really). Reading. Time with family. Your body doesn't distinguish between running from a predator and running from a deadline. It just knows it's under threat.

What about cardio? Jim's strength training sessions, performed with appropriate intensity, provided significant cardiovascular benefits. Daily walks brought his step count up from a sedentary 3,000 to at least 8,000 per day (probably the biggest factor in his reduced resting heart rate). He didn't need to run, bike, or spend hours on a treadmill, elliptical, or stair climber. His heart health improved as a byproduct of getting stronger and moving throughout the day.

As a quick aside, if you enjoy higher-intensity cardio, go for it! I personally love quick anabolic sprinting sessions with plenty of recovery and rest time. Many of you are into pickleball or golf. As long as you're prioritizing resistance training, walking, and not sitting, the rest of your activities are the icing on the proverbial cake of your fitness lifestyle.

The Result

What Jim discovered over that transformative year was that age isn't the enemy. Inactivity is the enemy. Poor nutrition is the enemy. Chronic stress and inadequate recovery are the enemies. But age itself? Age is just time passing. And time, it turns out, can be your ally if you know how to use it.

The human body is remarkably resilient. It can adapt, recover, and grow stronger even decades into life. Every cell in your body is replaced regularly: your bones every 7 years, your muscles every 15 years, your heart every 20 years. You are constantly rebuilding yourself, so why not take charge of your health and *become* the builder? With resistance training and adequate protein and nutrition. With consistent sleep and stress management. With patience, persistence, and the understanding that transformation is a process, not an event.

This is *how* you rebuild yourself.

But perhaps more important is the question: *why?*

Three months into his transformation, as Jim was finally able to keep up with his sons during a weekend hiking trip, something clicked. "For years, I'd been watching from the sidelines," he told me. "My boys would invite me on adventures, and I'd find excuses not to go. Too tired, too busy, too whatever. But really, I was embarrassed. I couldn't keep up with my teenagers."

That weekend changed everything. Not because of the physical accomplishment, but because Jim realized what he'd been missing. The crisp air, the laughter of his sons, and the feeling of being part of their world again. Before then, his sons had stopped asking him to join them. They'd learned not to count on their dad being able to participate in their physical world. "I saw what I was becoming," he said. "The dad who sits in the car while everyone else explores. The guy who needs help carrying groceries. I was turning into someone I didn't recognize."

Jim's new lifestyle wasn't about getting stronger. It was about reclaiming his role as a father, as a partner to his wife, as a man who could show up fully for the life he wanted to live.

Jim rebuilt with purpose—the understanding that his physical capacity was directly connected to the man he wanted to be.

Today, Jim is 270 pounds, or 60 pounds lighter than when he first wrote to me. He's stronger than he's ever been, and his cardiovascular health rivals that of men half his age. His A1C level is 5.4%, his cholesterol profile is within the normal range for total and LDL, and his resting heart rate is in the high 50s.

But the real transformation isn't visible in any of these numbers. It's in how he carries himself, how he approaches challenges. How does he think about his future? Jim discovered that his body was capable of remarkable change, even decades into his life. He learned that strength isn't just about muscle, it's about the courage to challenge your own limitations. To do hard things that pay off, that build resilience, that transform your very identity as an athlete of aging.

"I used to think my best days were behind me," he told me recently. "Now I know they're ahead of me."

Final Thoughts

This isn't about turning back time. It's about refusing to let time define your limitations. Your body is more adaptable than you imagine, more resilient than you've been told, more capable than you dare believe.

The choice before you is simple, but not easy.

You can accept the narrative of inevitable decline, or you can write a different story. You can age backward, biologically speaking, by giving your body what it needs to thrive.

Start where you are. Begin with bodyweight exercises if that's what you have. Add resistance next. Focus on protein. Prioritize sleep. Do the "big things" first before worrying about the weeds (and the often-misleading information overload on social media). Be patient with the process and persistent with the practice.

Every rep you perform is a deposit in your future self's account. Every gram of protein you consume is an investment in your independence. Every hour of sleep you prioritize is a gift to the person you're becoming.

The best time to start was 20 years ago. The second-best time is now.

Because somewhere out there, another man is sitting at his computer, struggling with his weight or health or confidence, wondering if he's too far gone. Your transformation isn't just about you. It's about showing that man that his story is just beginning.

The weights are waiting to be lifted. The future is waiting to be written.

What will your next chapter say?

Philip Pape is a Certified Nutrition Coach, physique engineer, and host of the Wits & Weights podcast, ranked in the top 1% globally. As founder of Wits & Weights Physique University, he helps adults over 40 achieve sustainable fat loss, muscle gain, and improved metabolic health through evidence-based nutrition and training systems. Philip's approach blends scientific research, practical coaching, and data-driven methods to empower clients to overcome plateaus and build lasting strength, confidence, and vitality. Connect with Philip at witsandweights.com.

. . . .

CHAPTER 15

Is There Life after Work?

Contributed by Dr. Glenn Berger

If you are lucky, you are old—or you are going to get old. If you have had a successful work life, that is something to be very grateful for. But if that is over, or is going to be over soon, that can be very challenging. If you are not that old and you are getting pushed out of your work identity, that can be very painful.

So, starting with the good stuff, it's good that you are alive. But for many, it can be very difficult to transition into the post-professional part of their life. This book, and the following words, are here to help you with that.

I'm a psychotherapist and coach. Here are a few stories.

A guy in his mid-50s came to see me because he was experiencing overwhelming anxiety. He couldn't sleep, and his rumination was driving him, well, crazy. He'd worked for a financial firm for 30 years. He and his three partners built it from nothing, and now it was worth billions. About a year before he came to see me, he had been assigned a "coach" to help him create a "succession plan" for his company. He wasn't aware why, but this was when he started having his terrible anxiety, which led him to seek out my help.

As the months passed, he noticed that the coach was encouraging him to give up his own responsibilities one by one. It dawned on him that the succession plan was for him. This meant that he was building his own gallows. His partners never said it to him directly. They told him he could always have an office—and wasn't the money all he needed anyway? He had the sinking feeling in his stomach that he was being pushed out.

Understandably, whatever the motivations of his partners, he took this very personally. He was a scrappy kid who worked himself up from humble beginnings. His work identity was a huge part of who he was. The success he found allowed him to take care of his family, both nuclear and extended. As each part of his identity was amputated from him, he plunged into a depression.

Here's another one. I worked with a woman who inherited a retail company from her father, whom she idealized. She grew the company into a substantial brand. When the financial crisis hit, like so many companies, she couldn't pay her short-term debts, and the banks wouldn't give her any money. Instead of taking the sound advice of her partners, she couldn't let the business go. Simply taking the money she would get if she sold it meant betraying her father. She couldn't face the decision and ended up with virtually nothing.

One more. I worked with a man who was very successful on the creative side of the movie business. He'd achieved about as much as any human being could. When he came to see me in his 70s, he was in conflict. He was still in demand. He had a business that employed several people who were depending on his continued work. But he was tired. He was uninspired. He knew that his best work was behind him. He'd had some health issues. He was being told to take it easy. But what would he do, who would he be, without the accolades? What would happen to his legacy?

Underneath all these stories is one unspoken word—*mortality*. The end of our central roles in the work world points to the fact that we are one significant step closer to the end of it all. Of all the issues that one can bring into therapy, mortality is one that we can't fix.

So, what is one to do?

First, let's look through one lens to deepen our understanding of what is going on here. Robert Moore, an archetypal psychologist deeply influenced by the psychological pioneer Carl Jung, developed a four-stage framework for the lifespan of a man. (I would say that there are, and can be, parallels for women, but for now we'll go with his structure.)

Moore claimed that the four stages of a man's life are Puer, Hero, King, and Senex.

The Puer is the youth. Like the bumblebee, he doesn't know that physicists say he shouldn't be able to fly, yet somehow he jumps off cliffs and survives. The Puer is idealistic, takes risks, rebels against authority, and doesn't care about the contingencies of life.

The Hero leaves his home to go on an adventure, slay dragons, and win the princess. He seeks to prove himself through struggle, ambition, and external achievement—often testing his limits and forming his identity in the world.

The King sits on his throne and holds dominion over his realm. He represents stability, achievement, and benevolent power.

Finally, the Senex represents old age. He is the Wise Elder. He represents an inward turn toward meaning, legacy, giving back, and spiritual insight.

Together, these archetypes provide a powerful lens for understanding the psychological tasks and transitions of a man's life.

As individuals move into their post-professional years, many face a loss of identity, purpose, and social relevance—challenges that can be meaningfully understood through this lens of archetypal psychology. This shift often feels disorienting in modern cultures that prize material goods over contemplation and relevance over introspection. In a world that often discards and ignores our wise elders, there is no healthy model for this passage. As a result, people often struggle to relinquish their former roles because they don't even have the first clue of what they are supposed to do next. We all know the cliché: the man retires and dies on the golf course.

So what is the answer?

If you are young enough, don't put all of your identity eggs in one basket. Yes, to succeed, we need to dedicate a great deal of time to our work. And we may also want to have a personal life outside of our work. (Let's not forget the meaning of those relationships.) But there's still time to pursue avocations beyond the work you do for money. Be creative. Start a side hustle. Volunteer. Save us from tyranny. Learn something new. Grow vegetables. Make TikToks!

Or how about this one: start learning about the most interesting subject in the world—you. Go on a deep dive into making yourself the best person you can be. Start working on it now because, if you do, when you reach that Senex stage, you'll already have plenty to do.

If you are already there, I'll admit, it's harder. But why can't you teach an old dog new tricks? Who said? Read the last paragraph and start doing all those things now. The world still needs you, especially when it comes to preventing tyranny. And we can add a few more to this list. You can teach. You can mentor.

Common wisdom has it that philosophy is for the old. It is also said that all philosophies, religions, and arts are ultimately about accepting our mortality. (Maybe art is also about sex, but that's another essay.) Jung tells us that in the second half of life, our development turns inward, toward the spiritual. Yet again, we have no guides for this in our modern world. Even organized religion often fails to show us a satisfying way in this regard. So that leaves a few ways of doing this.

One is to—dare I say it in this phone-based world—read. Immerse yourself in the inherited wisdom of humankind from every era and culture. Here are a few suggestions: the writings of Ptahhotep from Egypt; the Greek Dialogues of Plato and Socrates; the *Nicomachean Ethics* of Aristotle; the Upanishads from India; The Four Books of Chinese Wisdom; *Grimm's Fairy Tales*; *Man and His Symbols* by Carl Jung. Go deep!

Second, work with an old guide, like me. It is important to have a place where you can dialogue about these issues, where it is safe to talk about decay and death with someone who gets it.

Third, find a group of like-minded seekers who don't just sit around and "kvetch," but can do something positive together, even if it is just telling jokes and laughing.

Of course, stay active and physical. Dance. Love. Walk in nature. Look out to sea. Get some perspective on eternity. You are almost there.

We can focus on the sadness of what we are losing, or we can find joy in what we have right now. Cultivate "appreciative consciousness," the ability "To see a world in a grain of sand, and a heaven in a wild flower . . . . "

Finally, let us work toward the thing we all want but none of us have: acceptance. Buddhism tells us that suffering comes from attachment. What we are most attached to is life—the thing we are surest to lose. And knowing that we are going to die hurts like hell. I sure ain't no Buddha, so I don't pretend to have let go of that attachment. But we can all work toward it.

When we get old, we don't have the same energy we once had. The Rolling Stones may not write another "Honky Tonk Women." Whether they should or not, the world may not be as interested in us as it once was. You'll probably get replaced by someone younger, stupider, and certainly cheaper. Maybe even AI. You've had a good run. At least there's nothing to be afraid of anymore. You might as well sing that song you've kept in all these years. You might as well work on that painting you always wanted to do but never did because you had to make a living instead.

Framing this life stage as an archetypal journey helps us see the end of your professional life not as an end, but as part of a vital transformation into a phase rich with insight, mentorship, and inner growth.

Don't believe what your boss tells you. We need you. The world needs you. Your loved ones need you. We need your wisdom. We need your love. You have something important to give. Stick around and give it.

Oh, and while you are at it, do what you can to save us from tyranny.

Dr. Glenn Berger is a psychotherapist, coach, author, content creator, recording engineer, and creator of the HeartFinders Self-Cultivation Course. Early in his career, he worked with artists including Bob Dylan, Paul Simon, Mick Jagger, and Frank Sinatra. In mid-life, he reinvented himself as a psychotherapist and coach, now practicing in Westchester, NY, and with clients worldwide. His memoir, Never Say No to a Rock Star (Schaffner Press), is available on all platforms. He is passionately married and has two great kids. He brings an artist's sensibility, cultivated wisdom, and deep empathy to guide people toward courage, clarity, and connection. Connect with Glenn at www.skool.com/heartfinders/about.

CHAPTER 16

. . . .

Your Retirement Impacts Your Partner and Your Family

Contributed by Dorian Mintzer, MSW, PhD

If you're reading this book, you're either thinking about retirement, are in the process of retiring, or have retired and are still thinking about, "Now what?" What's life all about? Who am I? Who are we? What's important to me now? What do I want and what do I need? What does my relationship with my spouse or significant other most need? All of these thoughts are related to the question of: How do I want to live the rest of my life?

Whether you're a single man or in a relationship, it's crucial to think about what's important to you and what's important to the significant people in your life. For this chapter, I will refer to your spouse or partner as *partner*, to encompass the various types of relationships in this 21st century. You may be in a long-term marriage, with or without children or grandchildren. This may be a second (or more) marriage or partnership. You may be in a newly developing relationship. You may be in a committed relationship, living together or not. You may be in a heterosexual or same sex relationship. You may be in a blended family with children from various relationships. You may have responsibilities for others, including parents, siblings, nieces, or nephews.

Are you and your partner both working or not? Are you dealing with an "empty nest" along with retirement-related issues? Are you and your partner on the same page when it comes to retirement planning? If so, congratulations! You may already be having these important conversations. If not, you may be like many other men who are avoiding these conversations. Maybe you start to think about "what's next" for your relationship with your partner and for your life in general, but get overwhelmed, feel too vulnerable and alone, and decide to put the conversation on the "back burner." You are not alone! Now that lifespans and health spans have increased, there are more potential post-retirement years than in our parents' generation, and many more options for new possibilities.

Now, in the 21st century, in contrast to our parents' experience, retirement is not a destination, but rather a transition or journey. It's helpful to think about what you are retiring *to* rather than just what you are retiring *from*. You're certainly not retiring from life since you potentially have many years ahead. And there is no "right way" to retire from your work. This transition is different for everybody. Some people are forced to retire; others want to continue working, but in a different way—perhaps not as much, or perhaps by using their skills in a new arena. Your retirement is a change in *your* life. How you negotiate it is the transition.

Like other transitions, there is an ending to the previous stage of life, then a period of "unknowns" (now often called the "messy middle"), followed by numerous possibilities for new beginnings. Even if you're ready to retire from your work, there may be some grief and loss involved. It may be the loss of your role and/or identity, the loss of connection and engagement with your colleagues, or the loss of status and prestige, self-esteem, and purpose and meaning that your career provided you. These feelings are good and necessary. In times of transition, we need to let go of something to make space for something new.

It's helpful to think about prior transitions in your life. Have you tended to have difficulty with the ending, with the middle period of "unknown," and/or with the new beginning? Perhaps all the phases were challenging? Self-awareness of how you felt during prior transitions can help you anticipate some likely stress areas in this current transition.

Your Transition Affects Your Partner

Although you're the one retiring, if you're in a relationship, your retirement will impact your partner and your family. It's challenging enough for an individual, but it can be more challenging if you're part of a couple. You and your partner may have different dreams, priorities, and interests. If your partner also works, you may want your partner to retire or change their work situation at the same time as you, but your partner may not feel ready to make that change.

You two may also deal with transitions in different ways. Ask your partner the same question you asked yourself: How have you handled transitions in the past? Which part(s) are more troublesome? Also, ask: How have you dealt with transitions of other people in your life? These simple questions can generate some interesting conversations and lead to greater self-awareness of how you and your partner handle transitions.

Through my coaching and consultation, I've learned that some men want to retire at the same time as their partner and others prefer to retire at different times. You or your partner may feel you need to continue to work in some capacity to not outlive your money, or to keep health insurance until Medicare kicks in. Health factors for you, your partner, or other family members may also impact your decision. Some men assume that what *they* want will be fine for their partner. That's not always the case, particularly with dual-career couples. I have heard many women say they don't want to live their husband's retirement dream and want their own, or to at least be part of the decision-making process. It's easy to feel resentment or anger toward the person who feels that your opinions "don't count."

Often, people have intense positions about things, and it's not unusual for couples to get caught in polar positions: win versus lose or my way versus your way, with the assumption that "my way is the right way." This generally is counterproductive and leads to tensions, anger, and often a sense of dismissal and perhaps invisibility.

My goal in this chapter is to help you think about your relationship with your partner as an important asset rather than a potential liability. It's helpful to open space for the *we* of your relationship. Instead of "my way versus your way," think about what a win-win outcome might look like—often, you each get some of what you want, but not all. Things won't usually balance out perfectly; the point is to make sure the result is not too lopsided because, otherwise, you or your partner may feel resentful and "taken for granted." I've had people tell me they don't have time for these conversations, while others say they don't know *how* to have them, or just want to avoid conflict. The key, though, is to learn how to talk together. That's what enables you to find opportunities for compromise so each of you feel some of your wants and needs are taken into account by the other.

The Couple's Retirement Puzzle

I'm a coauthor of the book *The Couple's Retirement Puzzle: 10 Must-Have Conversations for Creating an Amazing New Life Together.* I like the concept of "puzzle," since it's a noun and a verb. As previously noted, you need to initially "puzzle out" the situation for yourself so you create your own retirement vision. This is done by asking yourself insight-provoking questions. Encourage your partner to do the same, so you each develop your individual vision, and then, through discussion and compromise, you begin to create a shared vision that works for both of you. Just like a financial portfolio, your shared vision isn't written in stone and needs to be reevaluated periodically as your life and situation change. Self-awareness, flexibility, and respect for each other are key elements to make the partnership work.

The noun part of *puzzle* is the way our life is composed of a variety of "puzzle pieces" that vary in size and shape for each of us. Probably the two most important puzzle pieces are finances and health and wellness, since they impact many other lifestyle options. Your puzzle pieces of life won't fit perfectly like a jigsaw puzzle, but they impact each other. Although financial issues aren't in this chapter, they are an important conversation to have with your partner.

In my book, the 10 must-have conversations to have with your partner are:

- If, When, and How to Retire
- Finances without Fighting
- Changing Roles and Identities
- Time Together and Time Apart
- Intimacy, Romance, and Sexuality
- Relationships with Family
- Health and Wellness
- Choosing Where and How to Live
- Social Life, Friends, and Community
- Purpose, Meaning, and Giving Back.

I'd also add the following to the list:

- Spirituality
- End-of-Life Issues and Wishes
- Legacy—Both Tangible and Intangible: How Do You Want to Be Remembered?

It's helpful to make two copies of this list, so you and your partner each have a copy. If some of the questions don't relate to you, that's fine. Concentrate on the ones that do. Write *yes* next to topics on the list that are important to you, that you've talked to your partner about, and that you and your partner have reached an agreement about the topic. Write *no* next to topics that don't meet these criteria. Have your partner do the same on their copy of the list.

Then sit down and compare your two lists. Doing this can sometimes produce surprises and lead to conversations. Sometimes one member of a couple may say we've talked about it, and the other will disagree. Or different topics may be important to each of you. Again, there is no right or wrong. Sometimes it's helpful to pick one of the topics you both agreed you've talked about, and discuss what's important to each of you now. If possible, put away judgments. Try to share and listen to each other.

People often feel overwhelmed about how to have these conversations. I want to give you a few starter points. In my book, I use the acronym **BLAST**, and say, "Have a **BLAST** in these conversations." Let me explain.

The *B* is that blaming gets in the way. Try to use what are called "I" statements, such as "I'm thinking" or "I'd like to discuss." Do your best to avoid "You" statements and words, such as *always* or *never*. "You" statements, even if not meant that way, can be heard as blaming and shaming. And, if you feel attacked, blamed, or shamed, it's easy to get defensive and react. This can lead to getting into a "reactive dance" with your partner, where you're both defensive and move into the "polar positions" I mentioned previously. This is usually counterproductive. Try to keep the win-win concept in mind.

The *L* is for listen consciously and intentionally, often called "active listening." Listen without interrupting. None of us is born a good listener. If you've been with your partner for a long time, you may hear the first few words and assume you know where the conversation is going. You may be right, but you may also be wrong. You can't know for sure unless you let them finish. It's easy to hear the beginning, assume you know what will be said, and perhaps interrupt, or stop listening and begin to think of your brilliant response.

A helpful listening technique is called "mirroring." Before you respond, literally say, "This is what I heard you say," repeating the words that you heard, not interpreting them. You may have heard it all, or part of it, or forgotten it all. This gives your partner a chance to say something like, "You got part of it but missed this; let me say this part again." Or "I think you're interpreting what I said, this is what I said." And then you can respond, and it's your partner's turn to mirror back. It can seem tedious, but it's actually very helpful to get you both to focus and begin to fully listen to each other.

The *A* has a number of meanings, including assumptions, appreciation of what you're hearing, and agreeing to disagree. Be careful of assumptions; they can get you into hot water. For example, without any conversations, you may assume your partner will agree with what you want. If that's not the case, you may be in for a big disappointment and perhaps a fight. Also, appreciate what you're hearing, even if you don't agree. You may need to agree to disagree. A helpful question may be, "Tell me why this is important to you." I recall at one of my first couple's workshops, the wife mentioned she had never asked her husband why something was important. Once she understood, she wanted to help make it happen. So, learn to listen and appreciate what you hear from your partner, agree to disagree if necessary, and don't make assumptions and then assume that's the reality.

The *S* is another action step. If you're not used to talking together about potentially difficult topics, **set** a **s**hort time as a **s**tart to the conversation. For example, you may use an "I" statement and say, "I've have been thinking, 'What's next?', and want to talk. How about setting up a time for a 10- to 15-minute conversation? We can start the conversation and come back to it later." By suggesting a couple of possible times to talk, you give your partner some choice and control.

The *T* also has a few meanings. The beauty of a relationship is that you can come back to it and **talk** in smaller chunks of time. Also, when you're talking, **turn** off phones, the TV, computers, etc., so you can be present and stay focused on each other and on the conversation.

Using these communication tips can help you begin to create a shared retirement vision with your partner. It allows you to discuss important topics, such as the timing of retirement, expectations of each other, each of your needs for some "alone" time for your own interests and friends, as well as "us" time. As mentioned, making assumptions and thinking you know what your partner wants can lead to disappointment, frustration, and anger. For example, if you expect your partner to do everything with and for you, you may be disappointed and upset that they don't want to change their life just because you're home more. Many partners say they don't want to be social secretaries and initiate everything. How might your roles change if you're not working or are working less? You may have one view, and your partner has another view.

There are also issues about intimacy, romance, and sexuality. Our bodies, as well as our libido, often change as we age or as health issues develop. These can be difficult but important conversations to have with each other. We need touch and intimacy throughout our lives, and being retired or getting older doesn't change that. But what may change is how we express love and intimacy.

Even in the best relationships, we need connections with other people. You and your partner may differ in your wishes for social connections and interactions. In addition, you may have different notions of your responsibilities for and obligations to family members. This may be further complicated if you're in a new relationship or blended family, or if some or all of your parents are still alive.

The issue of where to live may be a challenge. There are many more options than in the past. If you want to age in place, have you discussed what you need to do to make your home adaptable for changing health needs? Or, if you want to downsize, where would you move to? In addition, differing values and priorities may influence your preferences. If you want to live closer to any of your adult children, you may also want to have conversations with them about their expectations, so you don't set up any of you to be disappointed.

Many other topics may present themselves. Some people, in their reflection and deepening self-awareness, may turn to spirituality or religion. You may or may not be in sync with your partner on this front. Other issues may include health and wellness, end-of-life considerations, and wishes. Legacy is another topic. We all want to be remembered, in big or small ways. Legacy isn't just about a money legacy. The longer we live, the greater the possibility that we will either be a caregiver or need some caregiving help. This may be difficult, but it is important to discuss. In a similar way, people often want to delay conversations about end-of-life issues and wishes since it feels difficult to think ahead to that stage of life. But the reality is that it's an act of love and liberating not to shy away from these conversations. When a crisis happens with sudden health changes or death, it becomes a crisis on top of a crisis if you don't know what your partner wants. In this case, the conversation is important, but you also need written documentation of end-of-life directives.

I'd like to suggest a short communication exercise to help you and your partner communicate more effectively.

Step 1: I suggest you each think about your own patterns and habits regarding how you communicate with each other. What's working? What isn't working? Consider: What do I need to change to connect more effectively with my partner?

Step 2: Take turns sharing your responses. Make a list of steps you'll each take, individually and together, to both improve your conversation and support each other as you each work to improve your communication. Pick two or three items from your list that you want to work on. For example, I'll work on not interrupting when you're talking, or I'll turn off my phone or computer when we talk so I'm present and listening to you. Or, I'll listen to what you say and not quickly interpret what I think I hear.

Step 3: Try to arrange your schedule so you can talk at least once a week and focus on what is and isn't working on how you're trying to talk with each other. Try to brainstorm ideas that might help you resolve what some of the issues are that are interfering with talking more effectively with each other. Remember that you're on the same team, and learning to talk together and compromise will benefit each of you. Good communication can lead to creative possibilities for this next stage of life and can lead to greater emotional connection and intimacy between you and your partner. The goal is to find the essence of the *we* of your relationship while still honoring each of you as individuals. It can feel challenging, but it's possible!

Dorian Mintzer, MSW, PhD, is a licensed psychologist. She's an executive coach, retirement transition/relationship coach, therapist, writer, and speaker. She integrates her life experiences, professional training, and interest in adult development, life planning, and positive psychology as she helps people navigate the second half of life. She is coauthor with Roberta Taylor of The Couple's Retirement Puzzle: 10 Must-Have Conversations for Creating an Amazing New Life Together. She owns www.revolutionizeretirement.com and hosts the monthly "Revolutionize Your Retirement Interview with Experts" series to help you create a fulfilling second half of life. She's been featured in a variety of media and has a TEDx talk titled "Embracing Your Bonus Years as a Time to Learn, Grow, and Evolve."

A VIEW FROM CHAPTER X

"Sharing and Listening" by Arthur Mack

There are issues and ideas that we, as Chapter X, need to consider. Here are a few:

Wisdom: How am I using the wisdom that I have acquired at this stage of my life? Am I being a mentor for my kids and, if I have them, grandkids?

Helping others: Similar to the preceding. Am I being a mentor to younger people and a friend to those who can't do what I can do, not without assistance? To be a person others can count on. To be a person of my word.

We need to learn and be open-minded when it comes to the younger generations that we have in our lives. We need to be patient and understanding while we share values. Again, we need to be mentors and supporters.

Sharing history: Let the younger generations know what we experienced, but in an educational way. At the same time, we have to understand that they live in a different world than the one we lived in. In my case, I want my grandkids to know about my parents and grandparents, but in a way that is informative and with the idea that we want the legacy to live on. For example, my grandkids' great-grandparents were Holocaust survivors. And my dad was a highly decorated medic in WWII who saved thousands of lives with his bravery. Seek to share information like this with younger people in a positive way.

While sharing, at the same time be a listener. Some of my most cherished memories and lessons are with adults who really listened to me as a young child. There were very few, but I remember the ones who listened.

I believe the things I just listed are part of the key to a successful life in Chapter X.

CHAPTER 17

. . . .

Resilience

> **"Our greatest glory is not in never falling,**
> **but in rising every time we fall."**
> —*Confucius, Chinese philosopher*

Resilience is that transformational life force that allows you to get up when you're knocked on your ass. Ok, so maybe that's not the scientific definition, but you get the point. We only need resilience when we find ourselves on the wrong side of our expectations or when life has other plans we didn't ask for or count on. I talked earlier about resilience as a go-to tool for success. We've all been knocked down and disappointed. We've all failed, struggled, and met defeat head-on throughout our lifetime. But for every battle fought, we've come away smarter, stronger, and better equipped.

I remember when my son was around 10 years old and failed to make the traveling soccer team. He was small for his age but had an uncanny knack for passing the ball to the open player. His small stature deprived him of a powerful leg kick that the other, taller players possessed. He was bitterly disappointed, and it was a perfect opportunity to talk about channeling his anger and frustration into something positive. I suggested he use the next season to focus on his speed and ball handling and work towards the next opportunity. It was a period of maturation for him. He came to recognize that things happen, things beyond his control, and that he needs to deal with them. Moping and anger don't create positive outcomes. As I've watched him in his young life, I am in awe of his ability to bounce back from challenges. Now, as he nears his 40th birthday, he continues to be a model of resilience, having had to deal with the stresses of work and family, yet still retaining an amazing sense of humor and a fierce dedication to his values.

The resilience muscle, which you've carefully exercised, is the most important tool in navigating the next chapter in your life. Resilience shows up when facing uncertainty, when entering a transition, when the "you-know-what" hits the fan. If you pick your head up out of the foxhole of fear, you will see clearly that the road ahead is unlikely to be like a strip of newly laid asphalt. As we age, the challenges increase as we use up our allotted time. (Gee, that was nicely put.) You're gonna need resilience to climb out of that foxhole and move forward.

While our goal on this road is to use our remaining time in good health, vibrancy, and joy, undoubtedly, there will be obstacles. Some will be small and require little attention; you might just step over or around them. But others might be horrendous, where you'll need all your self-awareness, sense of purpose, and flexibility to get through. We are walking into a phase of life where disability, decrepitude, and death lurk. Is resilience important? In the memorable words of Dick Martin, "You bet your bippy!" I remember my grandmother, who, as she was feeling the effects of a hard life, decried, "When I meet God, I'm going to tell him what he can do with his 'old age.'"

I'm not going to try to pedal the idea that we're all destined to live great, healthy, vibrant, and exciting lives and then one day just not wake up. The road ahead is rocky at best. Which only drives the point that you have no time to wallow, no time to sit in front of the TV news feeling like life is not worth living, no time to do anything but fire up your brain, engage your body, and live every day with gratitude for health and everything you value.

This makes me think of a former client, now friend, who had been planning for life after retirement. His wife had suffered from multiple sclerosis for years and had become increasingly limited. They were seriously contemplating moving to Northern California, where winters were not severe and the more temperate climate was more favorable to her health. Unfortunately, her health deteriorated, and she passed away before the move took place. It was a very challenging time for my friend, who deeply mourned the loss of his wife. The life he had planned for his wife and himself was gone. His future was now unclear and directionless.

But he persevered. Time passed, and he met someone with whom he felt comfortable. They are now engaged, and he has, with the new relationship, acquired grandchildren. He never expected his life to unfold this way, but his resilient nature— his ability to fight through the gloom, one step at a time—has brought him happiness and a new, unexpected chapter in life.

Suppose your RQ (resilience quotient) is on the low side. In that case, I want you to go back to the resilience exercise in Chapter 5 and think about all the times you've picked yourself up and kept going. How impediments to success led to your inner strength, competence, and confidence in your ability to move forward. I want you to notice where the causes of your "defeats" came from. Were they due to something you did or didn't do, or due to some outside influence that you didn't see coming (or could never have accounted for)?

You can plan, plot, and put the wheels in motion for life after career, but a good portion of what happens to you and those in your circle is pretty much out of your control. You can do all the right things, and still, stuff will inevitably happen to throw a monkey wrench in your life. So don't throw your hands up and walk away—it isn't that bad. The solution is plain: you need a Plan B and maybe even a Plan C.

My daughter is a perfect example of resilience. The birth of her second child came unexpectedly during COVID. Complications forced an early delivery of a one-pound, seven-ounce micro-preemie, our Laila. She spent 97 days in the NICU before coming home. Meanwhile, my daughter, dealing with all the COVID restrictions, being a great mother to her first daughter (our Sophia), and running back and forth to the NICU, was a monumental show of resilience after having a C-section and dealing with the physical and emotional parts of recovery. I don't know how she did it, but she is heroic in my eyes.

While failure is usually viewed as a negative, let me tell you it most certainly is also the fuel for positive change. If the resilience just isn't there, then, of course, you do have the choice to say, "Well, that didn't work. I guess I'm done!" But that seems like a lost opportunity. Actually, more than that: a death sentence. Over my career, I had hundreds of conversations with men who had a very limited view of their life after work (it usually involved golf). My response was always the same, "What are you going to do if it's raining, or your back is out, or you need a knee replacement? Are you going to spend the rest of your life watching reruns of *The Golden Girls?*" These guys didn't seem able to turn setbacks into positives. They seemed helpless. They didn't have even the beginnings of a Plan B. It might be a lack of imagination or fear of straying outside of the comfort zone. Either way, it creates a narrow crevice of existence that limits the opportunity for exploration and joy.

What might you do if you can't do something due to physical restrictions? Life can't come to a crashing halt because you can't do that one thing, regardless of how joyful it is. You're an experienced human being, with lots of tools and, even now, a whole lot of potential ahead of you. It's time to open your mind to new possibilities that might be interesting, fun, meaningful, and joyful (remember, joyful is vital!).

A few summers ago, I had the pleasure of meeting Mario Bofill while on vacation in Hungary. He was recently retired and told me about his passion for golf. When I asked him if he had a Plan B, he looked at me like the proverbial deer in the headlights. I obviously touched a nerve. As we got to know each other a bit better, he shared his love of cars and how he was restoring one. It was a passion. He also talked about his family and his commitment to helping those he cares about. I was lucky enough to have Mario on one of my podcasts. He is passion-driven and sorted out his Plan B with great focus and clarity. He knows who he is and what he cares about.

I have to admit something. The idea of not being able to do something you love is hard to get your arms around, especially if you're healthy. It's a big ask and hard to confront, but it's to your benefit to try to imagine the impact of losing something you love to do. Imagine the sadness, the loss, the depression, all the emotions that stem from the loss. Have you ever experienced anything similar, like losing your job, being denied a deserved promotion, or suffering a physical injury that prevented your ability to engage?

Chances are, you've experienced enough to be able to "touch" the emotion attached to the loss. What did you do then? How did you deal with that challenge? How did you prevail? What supported you? Remember, you've been through a ton of experiences in your lifetime that were not all pleasant or wanted. But you got through it because that's who you are. Think about the process of digging deep inside to grab that resilience muscle to rebound. Sometimes your internal muscle memory is enough, and other times you might need to push through the challenge simply because you need to model your behavior for others (like children or grandchildren).

As you embark on your next chapter, keep the tools you've spent a lifetime creating close at hand. Challenges are meant to be overcome; mental toughness and determination are needed to recognize these situations for what they are. You can do it!

A VIEW FROM CHAPTER

"Avoiding Retirement Malaise" by Rick Shelby

Having observed a number of friends retire with happy and positive thoughts of what the future held for them in retirement, only to become quickly bored, disappointed, and restless to the point that they subsequently decided to return to work, I became determined that I would not allow myself to become yet another victim of retirement malaise. That determination notwithstanding, I instinctively knew I needed a plan if I truly wanted to optimize my retirement opportunity. Thus, due diligence was in order, and for me, that entailed reading several books on the topic as well as scores of magazine and news articles on the subject. Concurrently, I began to think deeply about those things that are truly important to me at this point in my life, so that ideally I could devote the majority of the time that was now available to me to those things that I was most passionate about from a self-actualization standpoint.

I committed to completing a written plan by the date of my retirement, which had long been set for December 31, 2019. Based on my military service, I had long been a believer in the KISS ("keep it simple, stupid") rule, and, thus, chose to view my plan as akin to the hundreds of sitreps I had written while on active duty. For my plan, this meant that it would take the form of an outline rather than a written narrative.

In the end, I decided that there were four things that were of paramount importance to me. First and foremost, to spend more quality time with my family; sadly, something that at times had suffered during my professional career. My second highest priority was to pay closer attention to my physical and mental health and well-being. My final two priorities were social engagement and cognitive stimulation/learning, both critical to my ongoing futile effort to become the proverbial Renaissance Man.

Once the pillars of my plan were established and in place, it was simply a question of identifying activities and pursuits that animated the realization of my goals. Thus, for example, in pursuit of my goal to promote and enhance my health, my principal bullets included improved diet, more sleep, less alcohol, daily exercise, and meditation and mindfulness. Needless to say, simple and straightforward. I am proud to report that I actually completed my document well in advance of my retirement, and haven't yet had to make any substantive changes to it.

Here's the bottom line: have a plan and work your plan. That said, if your plan or any part of it begins to fall short in any meaningful way, preventing you from creating the life that you had envisioned in retirement, don't view your plan as a failed effort. Simply make whatever adjustments, large or small, that are appropriate to place yourself back on a positive trajectory. The age-old adage regarding proper prior planning clearly applies; it affords you the opportunity to derive as much joy as possible in your final chapter of life.

Conclusion

"And suddenly you know: It's time to start something new and trust the magic of beginnings."
—Meister Eckhart, German philosopher

It's hard to think about endings without thinking of beginnings, as each stage of development, each stage of life comes full circle to its conclusion. So it is with this book, but its ending is truly only another beginning.

Throughout this book, I have led you into the deep end of the self-awareness pool to find the treasures you need to continue your life's journey with greater confidence than you had when you started. I expect somewhere along the way you struggled to find the words, find the meaning, and find the answers to help you locate the North Star in your night sky.

Your work life is either nearing an end or is already over, leaving you to navigate completely new terrain that requires a good deal of reframing and reconfiguring, as what you've known for all these decades is no longer relevant. Over the course of our work together, you've been asked to recognize and appreciate, in black and white, all the tools you have developed since childhood and to think about how to use them going forward. If you're a problem-solver by nature, Chapter X is just one more problem to solve. It's all in the mindset.

I've asked you to reclaim your first day of work experience down to the granular details, all in an effort to remind you that, despite the fact that beginnings are filled with anxiety and a profound lack of knowledge, somehow you got through it. Looking back at who you were on that first day and who you are today should clearly demonstrate that change, while challenging and destabilizing, is just another competency waiting to happen.

Values are a cornerstone of life. They are what guide our thoughts and actions. Our value system is imprinted in our DNA through our families and experiences. I remember my father telling me how important it was to protect my sister (even though she was older). In an attempt to do so, I confronted a boy, who was older than I, who was hassling her. In my attempt to live the instructions handed down from above, I wound up with a bloody nose and mouth. OK, so maybe that wasn't the best example of living your values, but I'll bet you can remember hearing messages from your family about how important it was to be kind, honest, trustworthy, brave, etc.

I've spoken with so many men who believe they are ill-equipped to live a meaningful life after they retire. But with a little reframing and some contemplation—basically the stuff of this book—they come around to the idea that, yes, they have the tools; it's just a matter of connecting the dots of past experiences to come to that recognition.

One of the highest hurdles, for many, is coming to grips with the loss of identity and all the ruffles and flourishes attached, like ego gratification, social connection, accomplishment, and purpose. Going from knowing, pretty much, what awaits you each day (no, I am not discounting the many unexpected surprises that naturally occur) to a life where every day is a blank page is, admittedly, destabilizing. That being said, how full was your calendar on day one of your work life? It is my hope and wish that you will never be a "used-to-be," but a person who needs no title or honorific in your name.

I have a particular discomfort when someone's response to the question "What's going on?" is "same old, same old." It's probably because it seems so devoid of purpose, empty, and resigned to mediocrity and boredom. From my perspective, every day is a gift and an opportunity—a chance for you to decide how to live your life. And while life isn't going to be fireworks and rainbows every day, with proper consideration and knowledge of who you are and what you care about, the possibility exists for this time of your life to be filled with wonder, joy, exploration, discovery, and growth.

Perhaps the most challenging exercise this book asked you to write was the eulogies you'd like to hear from those who mean the most to you. It's a hardcore ask to put yourself in the position of writing about how others will remember you after your death. It takes guts to put the tip of your pencil on the paper and courageously and truthfully put words on the page. But in those words, you can plainly see your values and the actions that made them real in the minds and hearts of those you love.

Just like everything in life, you get out what you put in. The angst, anxiety, tears, and struggles in recalling your stories are there to help you move forward with greater confidence. They are tacit permission to live this chapter of life fully, joyfully, and honestly, and to live with gratitude. I've recounted stories of men who can't or won't face the realities of their decisions to keep working, to push away Chapter X. Many are just too fearful of what the next phase might bring, some are not honest with themselves, while others aren't willing to do the work and are cowed by the thought of change.

I've not promised that you will float into retirement without a bump or hiccup; to the contrary, I have made it clear that you will most definitely face problems and challenges of various types. But honestly, that's true of life in general; difficulties, obstacles, hurdles, adversities, setbacks, complications, and trials have been there since childhood and will continue until you die. As you've proven to yourself, you are a resilience machine and will do your best to figure out how to deal with whatever difficulties come before you.

Use the work you've done on our journey together—the exercises and deep contemplation—as foundational in crafting your action plan going forward. Use it to recall all the tools you strongly possess and to strengthen the ones that need some attention. Use your words to remind you of how far you've come and what boundaries are important for you to maintain. Use the Wheel of Life to keep track of the levels of satisfaction you have in the areas of life that are important to you. I suggest you revisit this quarterly or semi-annually to see what's changed and what needs some focus.

Remember how many times you've gone from novice to mastery—this is just one more. As I bring our journey to an end, I wish you joy, wisdom, and continued exploration of your true self and why you are on this planet. Your Chapter X awaits!

"We cannot become what we need to be, by remaining who we are."
—*Max De Pree*

Want to join the Chapter X community?

Visit https://michaelfkay.com/connect/community or scan the QR code to connect and learn more about the people and community that inspired this book.

APPENDIX: WORKSHEETS

Who Are You and What Do You Really Want Out of Retirement?

Who are YOU on the day before you retire?

_____

_____

_____

_____

_____

_____

Who are YOU on the day after?

_____

_____

_____

_____

_____

_____

What do you want out of your next chapter?

_____

_____

_____

_____

_____

_____

VISUALIZATION #1

Your First Day of Work in the *Real* World

Who were you on your first day of work?

_____

_____

_____

_____

_____

_____

_____

_____

What were your expectations?

_____

_____

_____

_____

_____

_____

_____

_____

_____

VISUALIZATION #1 (continued)

How did it turn out?

_____

_____

_____

_____

_____

_____

_____

_____

What were your expectations?

_____

_____

_____

_____

_____

_____

_____

_____

EXERCISE #2

Create Your List of Values

Accountability	Equality	Justice	Self-discipline
Achievement	Ethics	Kindness	Self-expression
Adaptability	Excellence	Knowledge	Self-respect
Adventure	Fairness	Leadership	Serenity
Altruism	Faith	Learning	Service
Ambition	Family	Legacy	Simplicity
Authenticity	Financial stability	Leisure	Spirituality
Balance	Forgiveness	Love	Sportsmanship
Beauty	Freedom	Loyalty	Stewardship
Being the best	Friendship	Making a difference	Success
Belonging	Fun	Nature	Teamwork
Career	Future generations	Openness	Thrift
Caring	Generosity	Optimism	Time
Collaboration	Giving back	Order	Tradition
Commitment	Grace	Parenting	Travel
Community	Gratitude	Patience	Trust
Compassion	Growth	Patriotism	Truth
Competence	Harmony	Peace	Understanding
Confidence	Health	Perseverance	Uniqueness
Connection	Home	Personal fulfillment	Usefulness
Contentment	Honesty	Power	Vision
Contribution	Hope	Pride	Vulnerability
Cooperation	Humility	Recognition	Wealth
Courage	Humor	Reliability	Well-being
Creativity	Inclusion	Resourcefulness	Wholeheartedness
Curiosity	Independence	Respect	Wisdom
Dignity	Initiative	Responsibility	Willingness to learn
Diversity	Integrity	Risk-taking	
Environment	Intuition	Safety	
Efficiency	Job security	Security	

Write your own: Notes:

_____   _____

_____   _____

_____   _____

_____   _____

_____   _____

VISUALIZATION #2
You Have One Day to Live

What did I miss?

_____

_____

_____

_____

_____

_____

Who did I not get to be?

_____

_____

_____

_____

_____

_____

What did I not get to do?

_____

_____

_____

_____

_____

_____

EXERCISE #3

Uncovering the Tools That You Already Have

What was an example, in your life and/or career, where you successfully demonstrated PROBLEM SOLVING?

_____

_____

_____

_____

_____

What was an example, in your life and/or career, where you successfully demonstrated LEARNING?

_____

_____

_____

_____

What was an example, in your life and/or career, where you successfully demonstrated RESILIENCE?

_____

_____

_____

_____

_____

EXERCISE #3 (continued)

What was an example, in your life and/or career, where you successfully demonstrated CREATIVITY?

_____

_____

_____

_____

_____

What was an example, in your life and/or career, where you successfully demonstrated COMMUNICATION WITH OTHERS?

_____

_____

_____

_____

_____

What was an example, in your life and/or career, where you successfully demonstrated FLEXIBILTY?

_____

_____

_____

_____

_____

EXERCISE #3 (continued)

What was an example, in your life and/or career, where you successfully demonstrated UNDERSTANDING PURPOSEFUL ACTION?

_____

_____

_____

_____

_____

_____

_____

_____

What are some OTHER SKILLS that served you in the past that were connected to your success?

_____

_____

_____

_____

_____

_____

_____

_____

_____

EXERCISE #4

The Wheel of Life in Retirement

Directions: This exercise will help you to assess your growth and development in each facet of life in retirement. It will also help you to evaluate the degree of balance and level of life satisfaction you are now experiencing.

Step #1: Place a dot on each spoke that indicates your level of satisfaction in that particular facet of life. Use a scale of 0 to 10, with 0 at the hub and 10 at the rim. A 0 indicates no satisfaction and a 10 indicates the highest degree of satisfaction.

Step #2: Now draw a line to connect the dots and create your life wheel.

Step #3: Evaluate your wheel. Is your life wheel round or does it show flat spots? Is it deflated or is it full? What does this exercise tell you about your life? Is your life balanced? Are there areas of your life that need attention? In what facets would you like to experience more satisfaction?

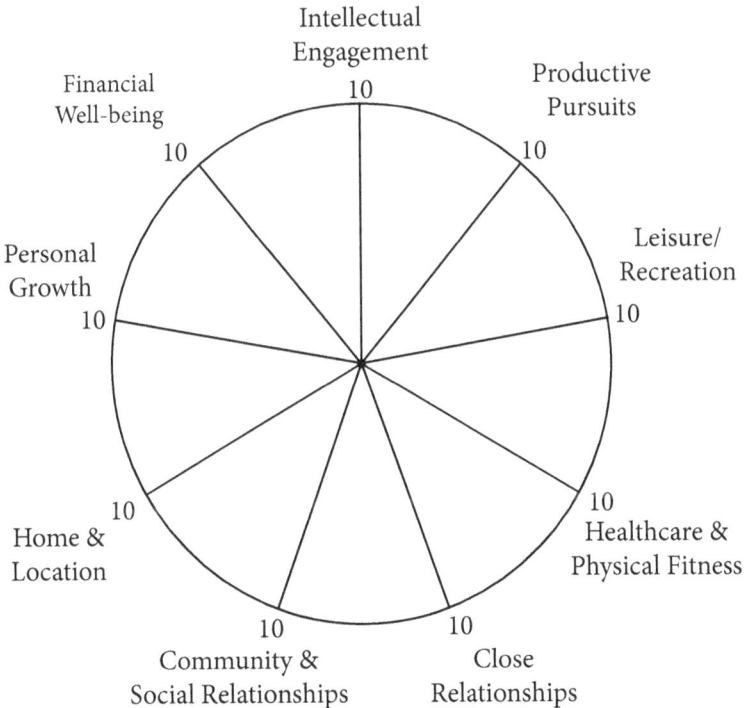

Download the full-size version of this worksheet from
https://michaelfkay.com/downloads/ • password: MYCHAPTERX

EXERCISE #5

Your 3 Dos and Your 3 Don'ts

What are your 3 dos?

_____

_____

_____

_____

_____

_____

_____

_____

_____

What are your 3 don'ts?

_____

_____

_____

_____

_____

_____

_____

_____

_____

EXERCISE #6

Generativity: How Can I Help?

Who, or what, can benefit from your generosity of time, knowledge, experience, resources, creativity, love, and passion?

_____

_____

_____

_____

_____

_____

_____

_____

In what ways can you use your generosity of time, knowledge, experience, resources, creativity, love, and passion that align with your values?

_____

_____

_____

_____

_____

_____

_____

_____

_____

EXERCISE #7

Facing Discomfort

What makes you uncomfortable?

_____

_____

_____

_____

What are the consequences of trying something that makes you uncomfortable?

_____

_____

_____

_____

_____

What are the consequences of NOT trying something that makes you uncomfortable?

_____

_____

_____

_____

_____

EXERCISE #8

Your Possibilities List

A space to imagine activities or endeavors that could bring you joy, spark curiosity, or feel meaningful. Use this page to begin your exploration.

What might be fun?

_____

_____

_____

_____

_____

What might be interesting?

_____

_____

_____

_____

_____

What aligns with my values?

_____

_____

_____

_____

_____

_____

EXERCISE #9

Getting Out of Your Comfort Zone

What are you willing to commit to that is outside of your comfort zone?

_____

_____

_____

_____

_____

_____

_____

_____

_____

_____

_____

_____

_____

_____

_____

_____

_____

_____

_____

EXERCISE #10

Who Am I?

Who am I?

_____

_____

_____

_____

_____

_____

_____

_____

_____

_____

_____

_____

_____

_____

_____

_____

_____

_____

_____

_____

EXERCISE #11

What Do I Value?

What do I value?

_____

_____

_____

_____

_____

_____

_____

_____

_____

_____

_____

_____

_____

_____

_____

_____

_____

_____

_____

_____

_____

EXERCISE #12

Write Your Eulogy

Imagine this person is giving a eulogy at your funeral. What would you most love for them to say about you, your relationship, and the impact you had on their life?

Your spouse/partner

_____

_____

_____

_____

_____

_____

_____

_____

_____

Your children

_____

_____

_____

_____

_____

_____

_____

_____

EXERCISE #12 (continued)

Your grandchildren

_____

_____

_____

_____

_____

_____

Your best friend

_____

_____

_____

_____

_____

Another person who is important to you

_____

_____

_____

_____

_____

_____

EXERCISE #13

Crafting Your Routine

	Mandatory	Very Important	Important	So-So	Not Urgent	Don't Care
Intellectual Engagement						
Productive Pursuits						
Healthcare & Physical Fitness						
Personal Growth						
Financial Well-Being						
Close Relationships						
Home & Location						
Leisure/Recreation						

	Action Steps
Intellectual Engagement	
Productive Pursuits	
Healthcare & Physical Fitness	
Personal Growth	
Financial Well-Being	
Close Relationships	
Home & Location	
Leisure/Recreation	

Acknowledgments

While it was my fingers touching the keyboard, this book would not have been possible without a multitude of people who offered their thoughts, knowledge, skills, and support.

First and foremost, I want to thank my wife, Wendy, who has been with me, with love and support, since we met that fateful night at the Rathskeller at Adelphi University in our sophomore year (1973) and are now closing in on 49 years of marriage. Your encouragement and love provides the fuel I need to do all the crazy things I do. Our journey continues with love and laughter!

To Elyssa and Mitchel and Rachel: you gave me three adorable granddaughters. Thank you! I love you all very much and marvel at your growth and strength.

To Sophia, Laila, and Eliana: you're the miracles in my life for which I am grateful every single day. I hope the hugs and kisses never end!

To the chapter contributors, David Bernstein, Philip Pape, Glenn Berger, and Dorian Mintzer: Thank you for your generosity, expertise, and commitment to helping others. I am the blessed recipient of your knowledge.

To the "A View from Chapter X" contributors: Bill LePage, Andy Abrahams, Michael Zeldin, Bruce Meisterman, Richard Eisenberg, Phil Wisoff, Phillip Bank, Arthur Mack, John Harrison, Robert McEachern, and Rick Shelby: Thank you all for adding your experiences. To those who shared their thoughts but didn't wind up in the final manuscript: I cannot thank you enough for taking the time to send them to me. Please know I tried.

To the beta readers and others who offered their sage advice—Richard Eisenberg, David Cohen, Michael Zeldin, and Meghaan Lurtz—your thoughtful counsel helped me think more critically and made this book really shine. It's a rotten job, but someone's got to do it!

My thanks go out to the professionals who helped me bring this all together. Kent Sorsky, super editor and cheerleader: thank you is not enough. Carla Green, who designed the covers and the interior layout: just *wow!* To Michael Tizzano, copy editor: thank you for knowing where to spare the reader from my verbosity. To Barbara Long, proofreader, thank you for your keen eye and willingness and grace to get the job done. To Mike Henton, my PR guide: I appreciate your knowledge and hard work! A HUGE thank you to my virtual assistant, Haily Greene, who kept all the pieces moving forward and being super responsive to my panic attacks! Finally, to Rochelle Moulton, who has shepherded me through my second book and stepped forward, after a bit of groveling and begging, to add her special flare and guidance: you know how special you are to me!

To all the podcast guests, writers, and thinkers whose work has influenced my own, especially those exploring identity, purpose, mindset, and later-life transitions: thank you for illuminating the path. I stand on the shoulders of those who asked bold and important questions long before I did.

A big thank you to Carol Anderson and Amy Mullen from Money Quotient for permission to use the Wheel of Life graphic in the book! You know how much you influenced my life and work! Thanks also go to Eduardo Placer, president of Fearless Communicators, for helping me organize and actualize my thinking into a cogent message.

Finally, to every man navigating the tension, wonder, and possibility of life after a full-time career: This book is for you. Whether you are stepping into retirement, redefining your identity, seeking meaning, or simply trying to figure out what's next, I hope these pages remind you that you matter, your story matters, and your next chapter can be the greatest chapter yet. As I am so fond of saying, *ab intra*, from within!

Thank you all for being part of this journey. May you continue to craft your life with intention, curiosity, courage, and *joy*!

About the Author

Michael F. Kay is an author, speaker, coach, and host of the Chapter X podcast, where he helps high-performing men discover meaning, joy, and purpose in life as they navigate the transition from career to retirement. Observing how these men (himself included) often needed help developing their post-career identities, Michael founded the Chapter X community in 2020 to provide them with coaching and a supportive network. Besides his time writing, speaking, and coaching, he has returned to his first passion of music after a 50-year hiatus. A former CFP, CPA, financial life planner, and entrepreneur, Michael lives in New Jersey with his wife, Wendy, and his Biewer Terrier, Phoebe. He loves spending time with his children and three granddaughters.

www.ingramcontent.com/pod-product-compliance
Lightning Source LLC
Chambersburg PA
CBHW071630140626
46555CB00022B/2049